Foundations

First Things for Followers of Jesus

Malcolm Webber

Published by:

Strategic Press
www.StrategicPress.org

Strategic Press is a division of Strategic Global Assistance, Inc.
www.sgai.org

513 S. Main St. Suite 2
Elkhart, IN 46516
U.S.A.

+1-844-532-3371 (LEADER-1)

Copyright © 1999 Malcolm Webber

ISBN 978-1-888810-61-5

All Scripture references are from the New International Version of the Bible, unless otherwise noted.

Printed in the United States of America

Contents

	Introduction	7
1.	Jesus – The Foundation of Our Faith	9
2.	The Word of God – Building on the Foundation	21
3.	The Authority of the Word of God	33
4.	The Canon of the Scripture	53
5.	The Ministry of the Word of God	71
6.	The Basic Doctrines	93
7.	Repentance From Dead Works	97
8.	Faith Toward God	109
9.	The Doctrine of Baptisms	131
10.	Christian Water Baptism	141
11.	The Baptism in the Holy Spirit	161
12.	Laying On of Hands	177
13.	Resurrection of the Dead	193
14.	Eternal Judgment	221
	Answers to Reviews	253

Introduction

When I was first saved, I knew nothing about the Bible and nothing about God; but God gave me a great hunger to know His Word. I would spend many hours every day searching His Word to understand more of the glorious One who had captured my heart and life.

The brother who led me to the Lord gave me a set of seven little books that I still have: *The Foundation Series* by Derek Prince. This set of books introduced me to the basic doctrines of Hebrews 6.

In this present volume, I have followed Prince's purpose and strategy. My purpose is to establish the new believer - or the older believer – in the basic "foundational" truths of Scripture. My strategy is to deal with the truths that Paul considered "the elementary teachings about Christ" (Hebrews 6:1).

My prayer is that this volume will be as helpful in laying a sound foundation for the Christian life in the lives of new believers as Derek Prince's small books were in mine.

Malcolm Webber, Ph.D.

> *For no one can lay any foundation other than the one already laid, which is Jesus Christ. (1 Corinthians 3:11)*
>
> *I will show you what he is like who comes to me and hears my words and puts them into practice. He is like a man building a house, who dug down deep and laid the foundation on rock. When a flood came, the torrent struck that house but could not shake it, because it was well built. (Luke 6:47-48)*

Jesus – The Foundation of Our Faith

In many places in the New Testament, the growth of the Christian life is compared to the construction of a building:

> *For we are God's fellow workers; you are God's field, God's building. By the grace God has given me, I laid a foundation as an expert builder, and someone else is building on it. But each one should be careful how he builds. (1 Corinthians 3:9-10)*

> *And in him you too are being built together to become a dwelling in which God lives by his Spirit. (Ephesians 2:22)*

What is the most important part of a building? The answer: its foundation.

The foundation in many ways determines the size, strength and character of the building that is set upon it. A weak foundation can only support a weak building. A strong foundation can support a strong building. A small foundation can only support a small building. A narrow foundation can only support a narrow building. A wide foundation can support a wide building.

The foundation in many ways determines the size, strength and character of the building that is set upon it.

Many Christian lives over the centuries started out well in the beginning but were shipwrecked in the end. Perhaps you have known some Christians who were once walking with the Lord and seemed to be very strong in their faith, but now they have lost their faith and are not walking with Jesus anymore. Perhaps you have even heard of some Christian leaders who have fallen. What happened to them? The problem was in the **foundation** of their lives.

The Foundation for the Christian Life

What is God's appointed foundation for our Christian lives? Paul answers this clearly in 1 Corinthians 3:11:

> *For no one can lay any foundation other than the one already laid, which is Jesus Christ. (1 Corinthians 3:11)*

The true foundation of the Christian life is the Lord Jesus Christ. Our foundation is not church attendance, dress codes, creeds nor doctrines. Our foundation is Jesus Christ, Himself, personally.

Jesus is our foundation.

The Nature of the Christian Life

The best definition of the Christian life is found in John 17:3:

> *Now this is eternal life: that they may know you, the only true God, and Jesus Christ, whom you have sent. (John 17:3)*

Eternal life, or the Christian life, is a personal relationship with the Lord Jesus Christ, and through Him, with the Father.

A personal relationship!

> *We know also that the Son of God has come and has given us understanding, so that we may know him who is true. And we are in him who is true – even in his Son Jesus Christ. He is the true God and eternal life. (1 John 5:20)*

Jesus came so that we could personally know God! This is also taught in the Old Testament prophecy of Jeremiah:

> *"This is the covenant I will make with the house of Israel after that time," declares the Lord. "I will put my law in their minds and write it on their hearts. I will be their God, and they will be my people. No longer will a man teach his neighbor, or a man his brother, saying, 'Know the Lord,' because **they will all know me**, from the least of them to the greatest," declares the Lord. "For I will forgive their wickedness and will remember their sins no more." (Jeremiah 31:33-34)*

Everything in our lives should revolve around the Lord Jesus Christ. We should go to church to experience Him in greater measure. We should serve one another because in doing that we are serving Him (Matthew 25:34-40). We should worship Jesus because that is our highest purpose as His people. We should live holy lives because that pleases Him. We should seek to lead others to Him so they too can know the joy and eternal blessing of a relationship with Jesus. Everything in our lives should revolve around the Lord Jesus. He is our reason for living. He is our Savior, our Lord, our King and our God.

Life Application Question

What should be the foundation of our lives?

How can we be sure the right foundation is laid in our lives so we will endure, grow strong and bear fruit that will remain for eternity?

The reason many Christians have failed in their lives is because they did not build upon the right foundation. They tried to build their Christian lives upon church attendance, denominational allegiance, or a set of ethics or doctrines. But Jesus wants us to build our lives upon Him – upon a personal relationship with Him.

The Word of God Points Us to Jesus

The reason we study the Bible is so we can grow in our personal relationship with Jesus.

The Word of God is given to man as a means to bring us to Jesus: to bring us to know Jesus; to bring us to experience Jesus; to bring us to a life of obedience to Jesus; to bring us to a fellowship of love with Jesus. Our knowledge of the Word of God should not be an end in itself. It should be a **means** to a greater end: the personal experience of Jesus.

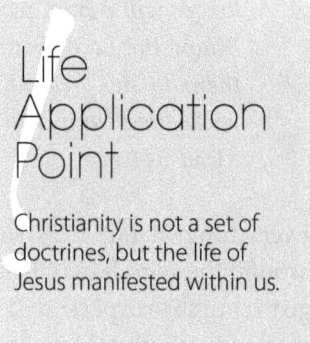

Life Application Point

Christianity is not a set of doctrines, but the life of Jesus manifested within us.

As we study the Scriptures, let us always keep this in mind: everything we learn should bring us into a greater personal relationship with Jesus Christ.

> *You diligently study the Scriptures because you think that by them you possess eternal life. These are the Scriptures that testify about me, yet you refuse to come to me to have life. (John 5:39-40)*

The Scriptures were given to us by God to bring us to the Lord Jesus that we might have life.

The Need for Revelation

> *When Jesus came to the region of Caesarea Philippi, he asked his disciples, "Who do people say the Son of Man is?" They replied, "Some say John the Baptist; others say Elijah; and still others, Jeremiah or one of the prophets." "But what about you?" he asked. "Who do you say I am?" Simon Peter answered, "You are the Christ, the Son of the living God." Jesus replied, "Blessed are you, Simon son of Jonah, for this was not revealed to you by man, but by my Father in heaven." (Matthew 16:13-17)*

Many men and women saw Jesus as He walked the shores of Galilee, but only a few recognized Him for who He was. It is the same today. Many people believe Jesus was a good man or a great teacher, but that is not enough. Jesus is the Son of God. Jesus is God Himself.

We know that is true, but we did not come to that understanding through study or learning. We came to that understanding the same way Peter did: through revelation from God by the Holy Spirit.

> **Life Application Question**
>
> How did *you* come to know Jesus?
>
> Was it purely through your own intellectual endeavor, or did Jesus *reveal* Himself to you?

This is how we will learn everything from God: through revelation by His Holy Spirit.

Jesus sent His Spirit to teach us:

> *But when he, the Spirit of truth, comes, he will guide you into all truth. He will not speak on his own; he will speak only what he hears, and he will tell you what is yet to come. (John 16:13)*

We must have revelation because our natural minds are not capable of understanding the things of God:

> *The man without the Spirit does not accept the things that come from the Spirit of God, for they are foolishness to him, and he cannot understand them, because they are spiritually discerned. (1 Corinthians 2:14)*

That is why Jesus sent His Spirit to teach us His Word and His ways.

> *As for you, the anointing you received from him remains in you, and you do not need anyone to teach you. But as his anointing teaches you about all things and as that anointing is real, not counterfeit – just as it has taught you, remain in him. (1 John 2:27)*

We should not ignore the teachers God sends us to teach us His Word. But, through the Holy Spirit we have a wonderful Teacher inside us who is well-able to show us everything God has for us in His Word.

> **Life Application Point**
>
> Just think: the same Holy Spirit who wrote the Bible dwells inside you to teach you that Bible!

After Revelation Comes Obedience

It is not enough to receive revelation from God about His Word. We must also obey it.

Jesus taught:

> *"Therefore everyone who hears these words of mine and puts them into practice is like a wise man who built his house on the rock. The rain came down, the streams rose, and the winds blew and beat against that house; yet it did not fall, because it had its foundation on the rock. But everyone who hears these words of mine and does not put them into practice is like a foolish man who built his house on sand. The rain came down, the streams rose, and the winds blew and beat against that house, and it fell with a great crash." (Matthew 7:24-27)*

If we learn the Word of God but do not put it into practice in our lives, Jesus said our lives will not stand the test of time, and the inevitable winds of trial and adversity will destroy us. A life that has been built upon the solid rock of Jesus Christ is a life that obeys the Word of God. James wrote:

> *Do not merely listen to the word, and so deceive yourselves. Do what it says. (James 1:22)*

If you do not obey the Word of God, James says you deceive yourself. If you think you will be saved and grow in the Lord merely because you have heard the Word of God, you deceive yourself. Hearing is not enough; you must also obey the Word.

Make a decision now that whenever God shows you something from His Word, you will obey it.

If you do not obey it, you will stop growing in the Lord, your relationship with Jesus will become damaged and your heart will grow harder to God. Eventually, if you do not change, you may end up forsaking God altogether.

Decide now to obey God. Whenever He shows you something from His Word, obey it.

> **Life Application Point**
> The truth of God's Word will set you free, but it sets you free only as you obey it.

As you do that, you will be like the wise man who built his house on the rock, and his house was never moved no matter what came against it.

As we obey what God shows us, we grow in our relationship with Jesus, we please Him, and we bear fruit that will remain.

> *To the Jews who had believed him, Jesus said, "If you hold to my teaching, you are really my disciples. Then you will know the truth, and the truth will set you free." (John 8:31-32)*

Do you want to be free? Do you want to walk in power with God? Do you want to grow in your relationship with Jesus? Then make a decision now to always obey His Word.

Summary

1. Our Christian lives must be built upon the right foundation for us to grow, to bear fruit and to endure.

2. The true foundation for our lives is the Lord Jesus Christ.

3. The Christian life is a personal relationship with Jesus Christ.

4. We come to know Jesus through His Word.

5. We can only know Jesus through His Word by revelation from the Holy Spirit.

6. After the Holy Spirit reveals the Word of God to us, we must obey it.

[Recommended for further reading: *To Enjoy Him Forever* by Malcolm Webber.]

Review 1

1. What is the most important part of a building?

    ☐ The doors.
    ☐ The windows.
    ☐ The foundation.
    ☐ The roof.
    ☐ All of the above.
    ☐ None of the above.

2. Why do some Christians, who seem to be so strong, end up failing in life so miserably?

    _____

    _____

3. What is God's appointed foundation for your Christian life? (Give a Scripture verse to support your answer.)

    _____

    _____

4. The best definition of the Christian life is:

    ☐ Going to church on Sundays.
    ☐ Being a missionary.
    ☐ Being a pastor.
    ☐ Trying to be good.
    ☐ Knowing Jesus personally.
    ☐ Trying to be kind to people.
    ☐ All of the above.

5. Write out John 17:3.

   _____

   _____

6. Jesus died so we can know God:

   ☐ Personally.
   ☐ As our Father.
   ☐ As our Friend.
   ☐ As our Protector and Provider.
   ☐ All of the above.
   ☐ None of the above.

7. Out of our personal relationship with Jesus comes:

   ☐ Worship.
   ☐ Holiness.
   ☐ Service to others.
   ☐ Evangelism.
   ☐ The whole of the Christian life.
   ☐ All of the above.
   ☐ None of the above.

8. Complete this sentence:

   Our knowledge of the Word of God should not be an _____ in itself. It should be a _____ to a greater end: the _____ _____ of Jesus.

9. We come to know God through:

   ☐ Faithful religious observance.
   ☐ Because our parents were Christians.
   ☐ Him revealing Himself to us.
   ☐ Our own intellectual effort.

10. Complete this sentence:

    The same Holy Spirit who _____ the Bible dwells _____ you to _____ you that Bible!

11. Please write "true" or "false" beside each of these statements:

    _____ It is good to know the Word of God whether we obey it or not.

    _____ Once we understand the Word of God we must immediately put it into practice.

12. Write out James 1:22:

    _____

    _____

The Word of God – Building on the Foundation

A personal relationship with Jesus Christ is the only true foundation for our Christian lives.

> *For no one can lay any foundation other than the one already laid, which is Jesus Christ. (1 Corinthians 3:11)*

But, once that foundation is laid, how do we build upon it? How do we grow in our relationship with Jesus and mature as Christians? The answer to this question is found in the words of Jesus, Himself:

> *Therefore everyone who hears these words of mine and puts them into practice is like a wise man who built his house on the rock. (Matthew 7:24)*

We build on the Rock of Jesus Christ in our lives by hearing and obeying His words. That is why we need to study the Word of God and apply it to our lives.

> *Do your best to present yourself to God as one approved, a workman who does not need to be ashamed and who correctly handles the word of truth. (2 Timothy 2:15)*

God's Word is able to make us strong as Christians.

> *Now I commit you to God and to the word of his grace, which can build you up and give you an inheritance among all those who are sanctified. (Acts 20:32)*

The more we know and obey the Word of God, the more we will mature in God, and the more we will grow in our personal relationship with Jesus.

Jesus Is the "Word of God"

In many places, the Bible calls itself the "Word of God":

> *And we also thank God continually because, when you received the word of God, which you heard from us, you accepted it not as the word of men, but as it actually is, the word of God, which is at work in you who believe. (1 Thessalonians 2:13)*

> *All Scripture is God-breathed and is useful for teaching, rebuking, correcting and training in righteousness, (2 Timothy 3:16)*

Jesus is also called the "Word of God":

> *In the beginning was the Word, and the Word was with God, and the Word was God. (John 1:1)*

> *The Word became flesh and made his dwelling among us. We have seen his glory, the glory of the One and Only, who came from the Father, full of grace and truth. (John 1:14)*

> *He is dressed in a robe dipped in blood, and his name is the Word of God. (Revelation 19:13)*

Jesus and His Word agree. They agree so perfectly that Jesus, Himself, is called the "Word of God". The Bible is the written Word of God; Jesus is the personal Word of God. The Bible perfectly reveals Jesus; Jesus perfectly fulfills the Bible. The same Holy Spirit who inspired the Word of God reveals Jesus to us through the Word.

Life Application Question

Do you see how important the written Scriptures are? They reveal the Lord Jesus Christ to us!

Therefore, the more we know and obey the Word of God, the more we will grow in our personal relationship with Jesus. So, if we want to know Jesus more, let us seek Him in His Word.

This, then, is how we build on the foundation of Christ in our lives: through His Word; through hearing and obeying His Word.

The Importance of the Word of God

Many Scriptures speak of the importance of the Word of God. It is said that those who attend to the Word hold fast to the Lord and to eternal life

> *Watch your life and doctrine closely. Persevere in them, because if you do, you will save both yourself and your hearers. (1 Timothy 4:16)*

> *See that what you have heard from the beginning remains in you. If it does, you also will remain in the Son and in the Father. And this is what he promised us – even eternal life. (1 John 2:24-25)*

> *…whoever continues in the teaching [of Christ] has both the Father and the Son. (2 John 9)*

while those who leave the Word forsake the Lord:

> *Now, brothers, I want to remind you of the gospel I preached to you, which you received and on which you have taken your stand. By this gospel you are saved, if you hold firmly to the word I preached to you. Otherwise, you have believed in vain. (1 Corinthians 15:1-2)*

> *Avoid godless chatter, because those who indulge in it will become more and more ungodly. Their teaching will spread like gangrene. Among them are Hymenaeus and Philetus, who have wandered away from the truth. They say that the resurrection has already taken place, and they destroy the faith of some. (2 Timothy 2:16-18)*

> *…as our dear brother Paul also wrote you with the wisdom that God gave him. He writes the same way in all his letters, speaking in them of these matters. His letters contain some things that are hard to understand, which ignorant and unstable people distort, as they do the other Scriptures, to their own destruction. Therefore, dear friends, since you already know this, be on your guard so that you may not be carried away by the error of lawless men and fall from your secure position. (2 Peter 3:15-17)*

> *Anyone who runs ahead and does not continue in the teaching of Christ does not have God… (2 John 9)*

The church of God is called:

> *…the pillar (Greek = prop, support) and foundation (Greek = stay, undergirding; from verb: to make stable, settle firmly) of the truth. (1 Timothy 3:15)*

We are commanded by God to seek doctrinal purity

> *Whatever happens, conduct yourselves in a manner worthy of the gospel of Christ. Then, whether I come and see you or only hear about you in my absence, I will know that you stand firm in one spirit, contending as one man for the faith of the gospel (Philippians 1:27)*

> *Do your best (Greek = give diligence) to present yourself to God as one approved, a workman who does not need to be ashamed and who correctly handles the word of truth. (2 Timothy 2:15; cf. vv. 19-21)*

and to keep the church free from error:

> *I urge you, brothers, to watch out for those who cause divisions and put obstacles in your way that are contrary to the teaching you have learned. Keep away from them. (Romans 16:17)*

> *As I urged you when I went into Macedonia, stay there in Ephesus so that you may command certain men not to teach false doctrines any longer nor to devote themselves to myths and endless genealogies. These promote controversies rather than God's work – which is by faith. (1 Timothy 1:3-4)*

> *He must hold firmly to the trustworthy message as it has been taught, so that he can encourage others by sound doctrine and refute those who oppose it. For there are many rebellious people, mere talkers and deceivers, especially those of the circumcision group. They must be silenced, because they are ruining whole households by teaching things they ought not to teach – and that for the sake of dishonest gain. (Titus 1:9-11)*

> *Dear friends, although I was very eager to write to you about the salvation we share, I felt I had to write and urge you to contend for the faith that was once for all entrusted to the saints. (Jude 3)*

If we live in "truth," we will walk in fellowship with Him who is Truth, and we will love Him with all our heart, soul, mind and strength. Moreover, we will seek to know Him in the fullest way possible, with our mind as well as our spirit.

What we believe will directly influence how we live.

> *And this is my prayer: that your love may abound more and more in knowledge and depth of insight, so that you may be able to discern what is best and may be pure and blameless until the day of Christ, filled with the fruit of righteousness that comes through Jesus Christ – to the glory and praise of God. (Philippians 1:9-11)*

> *For this reason, since the day we heard about you, we have not stopped praying for you and asking God to fill you with the knowledge of his will through all spiritual wisdom and understanding. And we pray this in order that you may live a life worthy of the Lord and may please him in every way: bearing fruit in every good work, growing in the knowledge of God, (Colossians 1:9-10)*

As we know His will, we will be enabled by His Spirit to "walk worthy of the Lord" and to please Him. Ignorance is neither pleasing to God nor profitable to man.

> *The goal of this command is love, which comes from a pure heart and a good conscience and a sincere faith. (1 Timothy 1:5; cf. vv. 3-4)*

Doctrine is not just academic. **Theology breeds methodology**. What we believe will greatly affect every aspect of our lives – for better or for worse. Correct theology will be expressed in holy, fruitful living. Sloppy theology will be evidenced by a careless, vain life.

A lack of truth is not simply a void. It is the presence of error. To those who believe doctrine is unimportant, let us say that in reality everyone believes one doctrine or another. If we fail to believe correct doctrine, we have by default embraced incorrect, or at least sloppy, doctrine. We cannot escape doctrine. Even in wanting to escape doctrine to be open-minded or in wanting to believe that doctrine is unimportant to Christianity, we are practicing a particular doctrine.

Proof of Our Love For Him

Since Jesus and His Word agree, if we love Jesus, we will love His Word. If we are truly submitted to Jesus' lordship in our lives, then we will obey His Word. Thus, our obedience to the Word of God is outward evidence of our inward love for Jesus Christ.

> *The man who says, "I know him," but does not do what he commands is a liar, and the truth is not in him. But if anyone obeys his word, God's love is truly made complete in him. This is how we know we are in him: (1 John 2:4-5)*

When John speaks of the love of God being perfected in this verse, he is referring to your love for God. When you obey His Word, your love for Him is mature. This verse reveals the truth that your attitude towards God's Word is your attitude towards God. You do not love God more than you love His Word. You do not love God more than you obey His Word.

How much does God's Word mean to you? That is how much God means to you. How much do you love and obey His Word? That is how much you love Jesus. There are many people in the world who call themselves Christians, and yet, they do not diligently learn and obey God's Word.

The measure of our love for God's Word is truly the measure of our love for God. Consider the words of Jesus:

> *"Whoever has my commands and obeys them, he is the one who loves me. He who loves me will be loved by my Father, and I too will love him and show myself to him." Then Judas (not Judas Iscariot) said, "But, Lord, why do you intend to show yourself to us and not to the world?" Jesus replied, "If anyone loves me, he will obey my teaching. My Father will love him, and we will come to him and make our home with him." (John 14:21-23)*

These verses reveal several things. Firstly, if we love Jesus, we **will** love and obey His Word. If we do not obey the Word of God, it only reveals that we do not truly love Jesus, no matter how much we **say** we love Him and no matter how often we go to church. Secondly, Jesus manifests Himself to us as we believe and obey His Word. Thirdly, the Father and the Son come in a greater measure to our lives, revealing themselves and manifesting themselves to us, as we obey God's Word.

This is a remarkable promise that as we love and obey Jesus, He will increasingly manifest Himself to us. That means our personal relationship with Him will grow and mature.

> **Life Application Question**
>
> If you say you love Jesus, but don't do what He says, do you really love Him?

The Greek word that is translated "manifest" in these verses means "to physically and outwardly present one's self to the sight of another" (cf. verse 19 of the same chapter). The word is used here to refer to an inward revelation of the presence of Christ, and obviously the revelation is a very **real** one. It is not some abstract and judicial theory that is in view here, but a real experience of fellowship with God.

This experience is not promised to anyone who merely identifies with Jesus or with His church, but only to those who truly love Him and obey His Word. To those who will abandon all for Christ and surrender to Him entirely, this is a precious promise indeed: a promise of the **abiding** (that is, continuous) and **manifest** (that is, directly and personally experienced) presence and fellowship of God.

> **Life Application Point**
>
> The more we believe and obey the Word of God, the more we grow in our personal relationship with Jesus.

This experience of the presence of God should not be confined to times of special prayer or church meetings; it can be our daily and continuous possession. Jesus wants to make His **abode** with us. Moment by moment let us draw near to possess Him through meditating in His Word and through believing and obeying His Word.

Summary

1. We build on the foundation of Jesus Christ in our lives by believing and obeying His Word.

2. The Word of God reveals Jesus. As we grow in His Word, we grow in Him.

3. The Scriptures are supremely important in our lives.

4. Our love for and obedience to the Word of God are evidence of our devotion to Jesus.

Review 2

1. Complete this sentence:

   We build on the foundation of Jesus Christ in our lives by _____ and _____ His _____.

2. We will mature as Christians by:

   ☐ Performing religious rituals.
   ☐ Knowing and obeying the Word of God.
   ☐ Watching a lot of TV.
   ☐ Becoming very good at sports.

3. Write out John 1:1:

   _____

   _____

4. John 1:1 implies that:

   ☐ Jesus and His Word always agree.
   ☐ Jesus and His Word sometimes agree.
   ☐ Jesus and His Word never agree.

5. Please write "true" or "false" beside each of these statements, and give a Scripture reference to support your answer:

   _____ Those who hold fast to the Word of God, hold fast to God Himself and to eternal life.
   Scripture: _____

_____ Those who leave the Word of God forsake the Lord.
Scripture: _____

_____ The church is the support and foundation of the truth.
Scripture: _____

_____ God commands us to seek doctrinal purity.
Scripture: _____

_____ God commands us to protect the church from error.
Scripture: _____

_____ What you believe has no relationship to how you live.
Scripture: _____

_____ If you love Jesus you will obey His Word.
Scripture: _____

_____ You can love God more than you love His Word.
Scripture: _____

6. Complete this sentence:

    In John 14:21-23, Jesus promises that those who will surrender to Him entirely, will experience the _____ (that is, _____) and _____ (that is, _____) presence and fellowship of God.

The Authority of the Word of God

> *Jesus answered them, "Is it not written in your Law, 'I have said you are gods'? If he called them 'gods,' to whom the word of God came – and the Scripture cannot be broken – what about the one whom the Father set apart as his very own and sent into the world? Why then do you accuse me of blasphemy because I said, 'I am God's Son'?…"*
> *(John 10:34-36)*

In this verse, Jesus quoted from the Old Testament, and He called the Old Testament "the Word of God." Therefore, Jesus specifically taught that the Old Testament was not the product of man, but it was from God. The Bible is God's "Word" or God's revelation. The Bible is God speaking to man. Both Old and New Testaments carry the seal of authenticity as the Word of God.

The Old Testament Is the Word of God

1. The Old Testament claims to be the Word of God:

   > *Your word, O Lord, is eternal; it stands firm in the heavens.*
   > *(Psalm 119:89)*

   > *All your words are true; all your righteous laws are eternal.*
   > *(Psalm 119:160)*

And the words of the Lord are flawless, like silver refined in a furnace of clay, purified seven times. (Psalm 12:6)

In the first year of Cyrus king of Persia, in order to fulfill the word of the Lord spoken by Jeremiah, the Lord moved the heart of Cyrus king of Persia to make a proclamation throughout his realm and to put it in writing: (Ezra 1:1)

... in accordance with the command of the Lord through Moses. (Joshua 22:9)

No less than 3,808 times in the Old Testament do we find the phrases, "And God said...," or "The Word of the Lord came, saying..."!

In the Book of Leviticus alone, the phrase "the Lord said to Moses..." occurs 35 times. Other examples of Divine inspiration are too numerous to mention. The revelation of the Old Testament was clearly given to men by God.

> **Life Application Point**
>
> Suggestion: look up "word" in a concordance. Also: read Psalm 119, the longest chapter in the whole Bible; every verse extols the excellence of the written Word of God.

2. Jesus gave testimony to the authenticity of the Old Testament:

Matthew 4:1-10. When Satan tempted Jesus in the wilderness, Jesus used the Word of God (from the Old Testament) to defeat him. In resisting Satan, each time Jesus commenced His answer with the words, "It is written..." and Satan gave heed to Jesus' words! The Old Testament Scriptures had the power to overcome him. Thus, Satan himself gave testimony to the genuineness of the written Word of God!

Matthew 5:17-18 (KJV). A "jot" is the smallest letter in the Hebrew alphabet; it is about the size and shape of an inverted English comma. A "tittle" is a smaller curl added to the corner of certain Hebrew letters to distinguish them from other similar letters. Therefore, Jesus is saying that the Old Testament Scriptures are so perfect and authoritative that not even the slightest alteration of them could be made!

Matthew 19:3-9. In answering a question from the Pharisees, Jesus referred to the Book of Genesis as authoritative. "Haven't you read," he replied, "that at the beginning the Creator 'made them male and female,'..." (Matthew 19:4).

> **Life Application Point**
>
> Obviously Jesus believed in Adam and Eve even if modern "scientists" don't!

Matthew 22:31-32. In answering the Sadducees, Jesus quoted from Exodus, and He said, "...have you not read what God said to you, 'I am the God of Abraham, the God of Isaac, and the God of Jacob'?..." Obviously Jesus believed the Old Testament was the Word of God.

3. Other New Testament writers called the Old Testament the Word of God.

> *It is not as though God's word had failed.... (Romans 9:6)*

The New Testament preachers and writers used the Old Testament Scriptures to preach and teach Jesus Christ:

> *For he vigorously refuted the Jews in public debate, proving from the Scriptures that Jesus was the Christ. (Acts 18:28)*

> *Yet Saul grew more and more powerful and baffled the Jews living in Damascus by proving that Jesus is the Christ. (Acts 9:22)*

The Greek verb translated "proving" in this verse means "to bring together" or "to put together": hence, "to compare and examine" as evidence and so "to prove." Here the word may well imply that Saul (a master of the Old Testament Scriptures) compared Messianic passages of the Old Testament with the events of the life of Jesus thereby proving that He was the promised Messiah.

> *As his custom was, Paul went into the synagogue, and on three Sabbath days he reasoned with them from the Scriptures, explaining and proving that the Christ had to suffer and rise from the dead. "This Jesus I am proclaiming to you is the Christ," he said. (Acts 17:2-3)*

> *For what I received I passed on to you as of first importance: that Christ died for our sins according to the Scriptures, that he was buried, that he was raised on the third day according to the Scriptures, (1 Corinthians 15:3-4)*

The following verses in Acts 17 reveal that the Old Testament was the standard by which the new revelation (which became the New Testament) was judged:

> *As soon as it was night, the brothers sent Paul and Silas away to Berea. On arriving there, they went to the Jewish synagogue. Now the Bereans were of more noble character than the Thessalonians, for they received the message with great eagerness and examined the Scriptures every day to see if what Paul said was true. (Acts 17:10-11)*

4. The Old Testament is replete with prophetic statements, many of which have already come to pass. In his book *Encyclopedia of Biblical Prophecy*, J. Barton Payne wrote that there are 8,352 predictive verses in the Bible! Many of these came to pass in the life, ministry and death of Jesus Christ.

Jesus consciously did things for the express reason of fulfilling Old Testament prophecy concerning Himself. For example:

> *"I told you that I am he," Jesus answered. "If you are looking for me, then let these men go." This happened so that the words he had spoken would be fulfilled: "I have not lost one of those you gave me." (John 18:8-9)*

Jesus began His ministry by quoting Scripture (Luke 4:16-21). During His life He fulfilled hundreds of Old Testament prophecies.

And beginning with Moses and all the Prophets, he explained to them what was said in all the Scriptures concerning himself. (Luke 24:27)

He said to them, "This is what I told you while I was still with you: Everything must be fulfilled that is written about me in the Law of Moses, the Prophets and the Psalms." (Luke 24:44)

Life Application Point

Suggestion: look up the word "fulfilled" in a concordance.

You diligently study the Scriptures because you think that by them you possess eternal life. These are the Scriptures that testify about me, (John 5:39)

If you believed Moses, you would believe me, for he wrote about me. (John 5:46)

A few examples of this:

> His birth at Bethlehem (Micah 5:2 with Matthew 2:1),
> His birth of a virgin (Isaiah 7:14 with Matthew 1:18),
> the state of the nation at the time of His birth (Isaiah 53:2),
> Herod's destruction of the children (Jeremiah 31:15 with Matthew 2:16-18),
> His flight into Egypt (Hosea 11:1 with Matthew 2:14-15),
> His return to Nazareth (Matthew 2:23),
> His ministry preceded by John the Baptist (Isaiah 40:3 with Matthew 3:1-3),
> His anointing by the Holy Spirit (Isaiah 61:1-3 with Luke 4:16-21),
> His ministry in Galilee (Isaiah 9:1-2 with Matthew 4:12-16),

His healing of the sick (Isaiah 53:4 with Matthew 8:16-17),
His rejection by the Jews (Isaiah 53:3 with John 1:11),
His use of parables (Psalm 78:2 with Matthew 13:34-35),
His triumphal entry (Zechariah 9:9 with John 12:13-14),
His betrayal by Judas (Psalm 41:9 with Mark 14:10),
His being forsaken by His disciples (Zechariah 13:7 with Matthew 26:31),
His being hated without a cause (Psalm 69:4 with John 15:24-25),
His being condemned with criminals (Isaiah 53:12 with Matthew 27:38),
His garments being parted and divided by lot (Psalm 22:18 with John 19:23-24),
His intercession for His murderers (Isaiah 53:12 with Luke 23:34),
His hands and feet being pierced (Psalm 22:16 with John 20:27),
His body not being broken (Exodus 12:46; Numbers 9:12 with John 19:36),
His being offered vinegar for His thirst (Psalm 69:21 with John 19:28-30),
His burial in a rich man's tomb (Isaiah 53:9 with Matthew 27:57-60),
His rising from the dead on the third day (Psalm 16:10 with Acts 3:15),
His ascension to the Father's right hand (Psalm 68:18 with Acts 1:9).

All these events in Jesus' life, as well as others, fulfilled Old Testament prophecies. Nothing less than the authoritative Word of God could contain so many accurate prophecies!

The New Testament Is the Word of God

1. Jesus spoke of His own words as the Word of God.

   Heaven and earth will pass away, but my words will never pass away. (Matthew 24:35)

Jesus, being one with God, perfectly spoke God's words (John 7:16; 8:28; 12:49-50).

> *Don't you believe that I am in the Father, and that the Father is in me? The words I say to you are not just my own. Rather, it is the Father, living in me, who is doing his work. (John 14:10)*

> *He who does not love me will not obey my teaching. These words you hear are not my own; they belong to the Father who sent me. (John 14:24)*

2. The New Testament writers clearly understood the authority of their writings and of their teachings.

> *Dear friends, this is now my second letter to you. I have written both of them as reminders to stimulate you to wholesome thinking. I want you to recall the words spoken in the past by the holy prophets and the command given by our Lord and Savior through your apostles. (2 Peter 3:1-2)*

> *All Scripture is God-breathed and is useful for teaching, rebuking, correcting and training in righteousness, (2 Timothy 3:16)*

Paul, in this verse, refers to "all Scripture" – both Old and New Testaments. "All Scripture is God-breathed"!

> *Bear in mind that our Lord's patience means salvation, just as our dear brother Paul also wrote you with the wisdom that God gave him. He writes the same way in all his letters, speaking in them of these matters. His letters contain some things that are hard to understand, which ignorant and unstable people distort, as they do the other Scriptures, to their own destruction. (2 Peter 3:15-16)*

By using the phrase "the other Scriptures," Peter gave "all" Paul's epistles **the same authority** that the Old Testament possessed!

> *For the Scripture says, "Do not muzzle the ox while it is treading out the grain," and "The worker deserves his wages." (1 Timothy 5:18)*

In this verse Paul quoted verses from both Old and New Testaments (Deuteronomy 25:4; Luke 10:7), and he referred to them as "the Scripture."

> *But what does it say? "The word is near you; it is in your mouth and in your heart," that is, the word of faith we are proclaiming:... Consequently, faith comes from hearing the message, and the message is heard through the word of Christ. (Romans 10:8, 17)*

Paul said, "the word...we are proclaiming" is "the word of Christ." Paul's epistles are filled with evidence of his conviction that what he preached and wrote was the Word of God:

> *Did the word of God originate with you? Or are you the only people it has reached? If anybody thinks he is a prophet or spiritually gifted, let him acknowledge that what I am writing to you is the Lord's command. (1 Corinthians 14:36-37)*

> *The Lord's message rang out from you not only in Macedonia and Achaia – your faith in God has become known everywhere.... (1 Thessalonians 1:8)*

> *And we also thank God continually because, when you received the word of God, which you heard from us, you accepted it not as the word of men, but as it actually is, the word of God, which is at work in you who believe. (1 Thessalonians 2:13)*

> *According to the Lord's own word, we tell you that we who are still alive, who are left till the coming of the Lord, will certainly not precede those who have fallen asleep. (1 Thessalonians 4:15)*

> *Finally, brothers, pray for us that the message of the Lord may spread rapidly and be honored, just as it was with you. (2 Thessalonians 3:1)*

> *for which I am suffering even to the point of being chained like a criminal. But God's word is not chained. (2 Timothy 2:9)*

John also believed he wrote the Word of God:

> *The revelation of Jesus Christ, which God gave him to show his servants what must soon take place. He made it known by sending his angel to his servant John, who testifies to everything he saw – that is, the word of God and the testimony of Jesus Christ. (Revelation 1:1-2)*

3. The Holy Spirit in us witnesses that the written Scriptures are the Word of God.

Just as the Holy Spirit bears witness to every believer that he is the child of God (Romans 8:16; 1 John 3:24), so He will bear witness to the authority of the Word of God. No argument can rob you of what is not only taught clearly in the Bible but is also the testimony of your own inner "heart-knowing."

Life Application Point

The Word of God is the Word of God whether you have an inner witness or not. But, isn't it a blessing that God gives us this inner "heart-knowing"!

The Authority of the Word of God

Since the Bible is truly the Word of God, it carries absolute authority. There is no authority in the universe higher than the Word of God. The authority of the Word of God is not limited by the extent of our understanding of it. It is **absolute**. The Word of God possesses supreme authority.

Life Application Point

The Bible does not *contain* God's Word; it *is* God's Word!

Jesus said, "...the Scripture cannot be broken" (John 10:35).

> *Your word, O Lord, is eternal; it stands firm in the heavens. (Psalm 119:89)*

> *... you have exalted above all things your name and your word. (Psalm 138:2)*

> *Heaven and earth will pass away, but my words will never pass away. (Matthew 24:35)*

The implications of this are as follows:

1. The Word of God is eternal. It never changes. 1 Peter 1:23-25; Isaiah 40:8.

   > *Long ago I learned from your statutes that you established them to last forever. (Psalm 119:152)*

   Therefore, anyone who preaches anything different from what has been revealed in the Word of God should not be heeded (Galatians 1:8-9; Revelation 22:18-19). The Word of God will never change. Any new truth that does not line up with the clearly revealed Word of God is to be rejected. The Word of God is the source and standard of all truth. Everything must be tested against it.

2. The Word of God is all we need. Human writings may help us, but they should **only** turn us to the Word of God. They are only of value inasmuch as they further illumine the Word of God to us.

3. The Word of God can be entirely trusted. We can build our lives upon the Word of God, knowing that it is eternally true and will never fail us.

   > *"Praise be to the Lord, who has given rest to his people Israel just as he promised. Not one word has failed of all the good promises he gave through his servant Moses. (1 Kings 8:56)*

so is my word that goes out from my mouth: It will not return to me empty, but will accomplish what I desire and achieve the purpose for which I sent it. (Isaiah 55:11)

4. The Word of God is **always** right (Psalm 19:7-11).

For the word of the Lord is right and true; he is faithful in all he does. (Psalm 33:4)

Your promises have been thoroughly tested, and your servant loves them. (Psalm 119:140)

Sanctify them by the truth; your word is truth. (John 17:17)

> ### Life Application Point
> The question is not, "What do you think?" or "What do I think?" The question is always, "But what does the Scripture say?"
> (Galatians 4:30)

Whether we understand it or not, God's Word is right. Always. The final word on every subject is always the Word of God.

Inspired by God

All Scripture is God-breathed and is useful for teaching, rebuking, correcting and training in righteousness, (2 Timothy 3:16)

All Scripture is "God-breathed". This term is much stronger than the English word "inspired." Good books or good music may "inspire" people, but Paul's meaning was not that the writers of the Bible were inspired, but that the Scriptures, themselves, were the very words of God "breathed" out by Him.

The Scriptures were not "inspired"; rather, they were "expired" by God!

In the past God spoke to our forefathers through the prophets at many times and in various ways, (Hebrews 1:1)

This verse literally says that God spoke to the fathers "**in** the prophets." The Spirit of God "in" the prophets spoke the authoritative Word of God through them.

> *...By your Spirit you admonished them through your prophets... (Nehemiah 9:30)*

The Hebrew in Nehemiah 9:30 literally says, "by the hand of thy prophets." God spoke to His people "by His Spirit by the hand of His prophets." This was how God delivered His Word to men. God did not inspire men to write something down. He moved upon them by His Spirit to write what He breathed out through them: His pure, infallible Word.

> *Concerning this salvation, the prophets, who spoke of the grace that was to come to you, searched intently and with the greatest care, trying to find out the time and circumstances to which the Spirit of Christ in them was pointing when he predicted the sufferings of Christ and the glories that would follow. (1 Peter 1:10-11)*

> *Above all, you must understand that no prophecy of Scripture came about by the prophet's own interpretation. For prophecy never had its origin in the will of man, but men spoke from God as they were carried along by the Holy Spirit. (2 Peter 1:20-21)*

The writers of the Scripture were not just "inspired" by God to write; they were "carried along by God" to write. Consequently, the Scriptures did not originate in the minds of those who spoke and wrote them down, but they were given by the Holy Spirit.

Jesus promised that the Holy Spirit would lead His people into all truth (John 14:26; 15:26-27; 16:12-15). The Holy Spirit moved upon the New Testament writers in such a way that what they wrote down was the exact, infallible Word of God.

At the start of his Gospel, Luke wrote that he had "perfect understanding of all things from the very first..." (Luke 1:3, KJV). The Greek word translated "from the very first" means literally "from above." This is the same word used in John 3:3 ("born again" or "born from above" by the Holy Spirit). This indicates the direct supernatural operation of the Holy Spirit. (Cf. 1 Corinthians 2:9-13; Galatians 1:11-12; Matthew 10:20; Mark 13:11.)

> *Now go; I will help you speak and will teach you what to say." (Exodus 4:12)*

> *The oracle of David son of Jesse, the oracle of the man exalted by the Most High, the man anointed by the God of Jacob, Israel's singer of songs: "The Spirit of the Lord spoke through me; his word was on my tongue...." (2 Samuel 23:1-2)*

> *Then the Lord reached out his hand and touched my mouth and said to me, "Now, I have put my words in your mouth. (Jeremiah 1:9)*

> *for it will not be you speaking, but the Spirit of your Father speaking through you. (Matthew 10:20)*

Written Down by Men

Men were the instruments that God used to write down His Word. In no instances did the message or the revelation originate with men but always with God alone.

> *Above all, you must understand that no prophecy of Scripture came about by the prophet's own interpretation. For prophecy never had its origin in the will of man, but men spoke from God as they were carried along by the Holy Spirit. (2 Peter 1:20-21)*

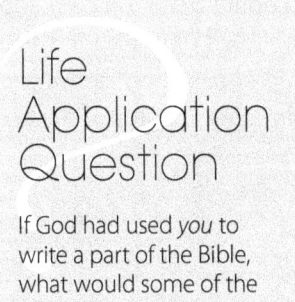

Life Application Question

If God had used *you* to write a part of the Bible, what would some of the characteristics of that part be?

The Bible is the "Word of God" and not just the words of men.

However, when God breathed His Word through His chosen instruments, He also used their personalities and temperaments, as well as their particular gifts and abilities in the process. In the written Scriptures, the individualism of the writers is seen as clearly as their inspiration. The Holy Spirit did not suppress the personalities of His chosen vessels and use them as "dumb channels," but He moved on and through the writers in such a way that was in harmony with their individual personalities and life experiences.

Obviously, since they were frail human vessels, not everything the writers ever said or wrote in their lives was inspired by God. However, their writings that became the Bible were **always** inspired by God and therefore infallible.

Preserved by God

> *And the words of the Lord are flawless, like silver refined in a furnace of clay, purified seven times. (Psalm 12:6)*

God made sure His words were given perfectly through the human instruments He chose to use. Furthermore, through the centuries, God has preserved His written Word in purity.

To doubt that God could do this is to doubt that "with God all things are possible"! Our faith in the integrity and accuracy of the written Word of God is based on nothing other than the power and faithfulness of the Almighty Creator of the heavens and the earth.

Summary

1. The Bible is the Word of God, both Old and New Testaments.

2. The written Word of God has absolute authority and is the ultimate standard of all truth.

3. The Scriptures were "breathed out" by God and written down by men.

4. The Scriptures have been preserved by God down through history, and what we hold in our hands are the very "oracles of God"!

Review 3

1. Jesus called the Old Testament:

   ☐ A good book.
   ☐ Jewish tradition.
   ☐ The Word of God.

2. Give two Scripture references in which the Old Testament claims to be the Word of God.

   _____   _____

3. In which of these ways did Jesus authenticate the Old Testament as God's Word:

   ☐ Jesus used the Word of God to defeat Satan.
   ☐ Jesus said no alteration of the Old Testament Scriptures could ever be made.
   ☐ Jesus referred to the Old Testament as the final authority on truth.
   ☐ All of the above.
   ☐ None of the above.

4. True or false? Several New Testament writers called the Old Testament the Word of God. _____

5. The thousands of prophecies in the Old Testament that have already come to pass, many of which concerned Jesus' life, ministry and death, prove:

   ☐ Nothing.
   ☐ Some writers of the Old Testament made some lucky guesses.
   ☐ The Old Testament is the Word of God.

6. Give six Old Testament Scriptures that contained prophecies concerning Jesus that came to pass.

   _____ _____ _____

   _____ _____ _____

7. Jesus spoke of His own words as:

   ☐ Sound advice.
   ☐ Not true.
   ☐ Human wisdom.
   ☐ The Word of God.
   ☐ Fables of man.

8. True or false? The writers of the New Testament believed that what they wrote was the Word of God. _____

9. Write out 2 Timothy 3:16:

   _____

   _____

   _____

10. Do you know in your own heart that the Bible is the Word of God? _____

11. Complete this sentence:

    The Bible does not _____ God's Word; it _____ God's Word!

12. Please write "true" or "false" beside each of these statements:

    _____The Word of God is eternal. It never changes.

    _____The Word of God is all we need for answers to all life's questions.

    _____The Word of God can be entirely trusted.

    _____The Word of God is usually right.

13. Complete this sentence:

    The Scriptures were not "inspired"; rather they were "_____" by God!

14. Who helped the writers of the Bible so that what they wrote was perfect and infallible?

    ☐ The Holy Spirit.
    ☐ The devil.
    ☐ The Pope.
    ☐ No one. They made up the Bible themselves.

15. Please write "true" or "false" beside each of these statements:

    _____Men were the instruments that God used to write down His Word.

    _____When God breathed His Word through His chosen instruments, He also used their personalities and temperaments, as well as their particular gifts and abilities in the process.

    _____The Holy Spirit suppressed the personalities of His chosen vessels and used them as "dumb channels."

_____Everything the New Testament writers ever said or wrote in their lives was inspired by God and therefore infallible.

_____Since the New Testament was written down by men, we cannot trust it.

_____The Scriptures have been preserved by God down through history, and what we hold in our hands are the very "oracles of God"!

The Canon of the Scripture

The word "canon" means "a rule, a measuring line, a standard." The word has been used by Christians since the fourth century to denote an authoritative list of the books belonging to the Old and New Testaments. Thus, the 66 books that met the standard as the inspired Word of God found a place in the Canon of the Scriptures.

Our Old Testament Canon includes 39 books, and the New Testament Canon includes 27 books.

The Old Testament Canon

Jewish tradition ascribes the Old Testament Canon to Ezra and the men of the Great Synagogue in the fifth century B.C. This tradition is based upon Ezra's zeal for God as well as his ability.

> *For Ezra had devoted himself to the study and observance of the Law of the Lord, and to teaching its decrees and laws in Israel. (Ezra 7:10)*

> *…Ezra the priest and teacher, (was) a man learned in matters concerning the commands and decrees of the Lord for Israel: (Ezra 7:11)*

Ezra was qualified to take the Old Testament books and determine their authenticity by the overshadowing Spirit. He and the men with him probably then arranged the books in their present form.

Josephus, the famous Jewish historian, confirmed the books of the Old Testament Canon when he wrote his work *Against Apion* 1:8 in A.D. 90, and he wrote:

> For we (i.e., the Jews) have not an innumerable multitude of books among us, disagreeing with and contradicting one another (as the Greeks have), but only twenty two books, which contain the records of all the past times; which are justly believed to be divine; and of them, five belong to Moses, which contain his laws and the tradition of the origin of mankind till his death. This interval of time was little short of three thousand years; but as to the time from the death of Moses till the reign of Artaxerxes, king of Persia, who reigned after Xerxes, the prophets, who were after Moses, wrote down what was done in their times in thirteen books. The remaining four books contain hymns to God and precepts for the conduct of human life. It is true, our history hath been written since Artaxerxes, very particularly, but hath not been esteemed of the like **authority** with the former by our forefathers, because there hath not been an exact succession of prophets since that time; and how firmly we have given credit to those books of our own nation is evident by what we do; for during so many ages as have already passed, no one has been so bold as either to add anything to them or take it from them; but it becomes natural to all Jews, immediately and from their very birth, to esteem those books to contain divine doctrines, and to persist in them, and, if occasion be, willingly to die for them.

Thus, the writings of Josephus tell us the number of books in the Old Testament Canon (22) and that the Canon was "closed" at the time of Artaxerxes (same time as Ezra and Nehemiah).

Josephus' 22 Old Testament books are the same as our 39 Old Testament books. His books were as follows:

5 Books of Moses	**13 Prophetical Books**	**4 Hymns to God**
1. Genesis	1. Joshua	1. Psalms
2. Exodus	2. Judges and Ruth	2. Proverbs
3. Leviticus	3. Two Books of Samuel	3. Ecclesiastes
4. Numbers	4. Two Books of Kings	4. Song of Solomon
5. Deuteronomy	5. Two Books of Chronicles	
	6. Ezra and Nehemiah	
	7. Esther	
	8. Isaiah	
	9. Jeremiah and Lamentations	
	10. Ezekiel	
	11. Daniel	
	12. Books of 12 Minor Prophets	
	13. Job	

The difference between Josephus' 22 books and our 39 books can be explained simply. He counted the Minor Prophets as one book (we count it as 12), he counted Samuel, Kings and Chronicles as one book each (we count them as two books each), he counted Ezra and Nehemiah as one book (we count them as two), he counted Ruth and Judges as one (we count them as two) and he counted Jeremiah and Lamentations as one book (we count them as two). Thus, Josephus' 22 books are exactly the same as our 39.

This separation of books happened at the time when the Hebrew Scriptures were translated into Greek. This translation was known as the *Septuagint* (from the Latin word *septuaginta* which means seventy) because of the seventy (some say seventy-two) Jewish scholars who were supposed to have prepared it. This translation is commonly denoted by the Roman numeral LXX.

The work was done in Alexandria, Egypt during the second and third centuries B.C. when Greek was the common language of the known world.

At that time the original Hebrew Scriptures were divided into the following 39 books of our Old Testament:

5 Books of Moses.	The Law.
12 Books of History.	Joshua to Esther.
5 Books of Poetry.	Job to Song of Solomon.
17 Books of Prophecy.	Isaiah to Malachi.

This same Canon was confirmed by the Jewish synod of Jamnia about A.D. 90. The decision by these rabbis to close the Canon of Hebrew books resulted from:

1. the multiplication and popularity of false writings;
2. the fall of Jerusalem (A.D. 70) created a threat to the religious tradition of the Jews;
3. the disputes with the Christians over their interpretation of the Jewish Scriptures in preaching and writing.

Four major criteria operated in their decisions:

1. the content of the books in question must be in harmony with the law;
2. the books must come within the time period between Moses and Ezra;
3. the language of the original books had to be Hebrew;
4. they had to be written within the geographical boundaries of Israel.

The Jews called the Old Testament *The Law, the Prophets and the Writings* (cf. Luke 24:44).

(The above is a simplification of a complex historical process. For further reading on the Old Testament Canon, please refer to a good, conservative Survey of the Old Testament, Bible Dictionary or Encyclopedia.)

The Masoretes

Before we leave the Old Testament Canon, it would be profitable to say a word about the Masoretes. The Masoretes (lit. *transmitters*) succeeded the old scribes as the custodians of the Hebrew Scriptures. They were active from about A.D. 500 to 1000. They were greatly concerned with the preservation of the purity of the text, and they established strict rules to be followed by all copyists of the Hebrew Scriptures. No word or letter could be written from memory. The scribe had to look attentively at each word and pronounce it before writing it down. The number of letters in a book was counted, and its middle letter was given. Similarly with the words, and again the middle word of the book was noted. They collected any peculiarities in spelling or in the forms or positions of letters. They recorded the number of times a particular word or phrase occurred. If any of these figures did not tally with the newly made copy, the work was discarded, and the task began again.

In 1948, a considerable number of very ancient manuscripts were discovered in a cave near the Dead Sea (the *Dead Sea Scrolls*). Scholars declared that these scrolls of Isaiah and other Old Testament writers were hundreds of years older than any yet found, dating back possibly to the second century before Christ. Many years of intensive study by the greatest Hebrew authorities have revealed only slight differences between the Masoretic text and that of the Dead Sea scrolls, a marvelous tribute to the faithfulness of the copyists, and a wonderful example of the truth of Matthew 5:18:

> Life Application Question
>
> Can you see how God was watching over His Word all through the centuries to preserve it?

> *I tell you the truth, until heaven and earth disappear, not the smallest letter, not the least stroke of a pen, will by any means disappear from the Law until everything is accomplished.*

The New Testament Canon

The New Testament books were written either by an apostle or a companion of an apostle.

> *built on the foundation of the apostles and prophets, with Christ Jesus himself as the chief cornerstone. (Ephesians 2:20)*

All 27 books of the New Testament were placed in the Canon after they had been treasured by the churches. The churches exchanged letters and copied them, and sent them to other churches. Only letters with apostolic authority were accepted as a part of the Canon. That means the letters had to be written by an apostle or by an apostolic associate.

As far as it is known, it was a letter of Athanasius of Alexandria in A.D. 367 that first listed the 27 books of our New Testament as authoritative.

The Council of Carthage, A.D. 397, said of the already accepted New Testament Canon, "Nothing shall be read in the churches except the recognized canon." They then named the 27 books of the New Testament. They also stated, "A New Testament book must be written by an apostle or an amanuensis (i.e., a secretary or personal assistant) of an apostle." So, by the fourth and fifth centuries, all our New Testament books were generally recognized and others excluded.

(Again, the above is a simplification of a complex historical process. For further reading on the New Testament Canon, as well as on the history of the English versions of the Bible, please refer to a good, conservative Bible Dictionary or Encyclopedia.)

The Apocrypha

The word "apocrypha" means "hidden" or "concealed," and the Apocrypha is the name given to a group of 14 books. These books were written between the first and third centuries B.C. after the time of Ezra and Nehemiah.

These books were never accepted as canonical by the Council of Jamnia in A.D. 90. However, the Greek Septuagint included these writings. Then, Jerome, in his Latin translation of the Septuagint in A.D. 382 (the *Vulgate*), also included these books in his bible (even though Jerome noted that these 14 books were inferior to the canonical books). For that reason, they have ended up in the Roman Catholic Bible (since the Council of Trent in A.D. 1546) providing the source for a number of Catholicism's serious theological errors.

None of these books claim divine inspiration; in fact, they include historical, geographical and chronological errors. There are also many instances in these books in which they teach doctrines that are contrary to Scripture. For instance, lying is sanctioned in some cases, magic is advocated and practiced, prayer and offerings are made for the dead, cruelty to slaves is condoned, the pre-existence of souls is taught, original sin is denied, purgatory is taught, etc. The positive value of these books is that they do fill the historical gap between the Old and New Testaments, and they give some insight into the spiritual, philosophical and theological ideas that developed between the testaments.

These books, however, are not inspired and are not to be considered part of the Word of God.

Early Church Literature

There are a number of extant works that date from the first two centuries, written by leaders and teachers in the Early Church (sometimes called the *Apostolic Fathers*). Some of these works are:

>The Epistle of Clement of Rome.
>The so-called "Second Letter of Clement to the Corinthians" which is not considered to be written by Clement of Rome.
>The Epistles of Ignatius.
>The Epistle of Polycarp.
>The (Account of the) Martyrdom of Polycarp.

The Didache (or Teaching of the Apostles).
The Epistle of Barnabas.
The Shepherd of Hermas.
The Epistle to Diognetus.
The Fragments of Papias.
Some writings from Irenaeus.

While these works are not considered to be Scripture, their primary value is that they give some insight into the life, times and doctrine of the Early Church since they were written by men who were there (for example, Polycarp was a disciple of John, the apostle).

The Pseudepigrapha

There is a vast amount of literature called the *Pseudepigrapha*. Pseudo = false; epi = upon; graphi = write; in other words, "to write upon falsely." This literature found a place in neither the Canon of Scripture nor the Apocrypha. It was written between 200 B.C. and A.D. 600. It was written under names such as Prophets, Kings or Old or New Testament names. There are 18 Old Testament false writings mentioned occasionally (the exact number is not known). There are more than 200 Pseudepigrapha of the New Testament. There are many false "Gospels" such as "The Gospel of Mary, of Thomas, of Peter, of the Twelve," and others. Much of the writing was apocryphal. No Canon or council recognized these writings. Eusebius, an early church historian, said these writings were "totally absurd and impious."

> ## Life Application Question
>
> Many books in the world claim to be "of God." Should we give them as much authority in our lives as we do the Word of God? Why not?

The Bible Is "the Scripture"

Let us look again at Jesus' statement concerning the Old Testament in John 10:

> *Jesus answered them, "Is it not written in your Law, 'I have said you are gods'? If he called them 'gods,' to whom the word of God came – and the Scripture cannot be broken – what about the one whom the Father set apart as his very own and sent into the world? Why then do you accuse me of blasphemy because I said, 'I am God's Son'?" (John 10:34-36)*

In the same verse that Jesus called the Old Testament "the Word of God," He also called it "the Scripture." "The Scripture" means literally "that which was written." Not everything in the mind of our infinite God has been written down. Neither has everything God has ever revealed to men been written down. The Bible does not contain the entire knowledge of God and His purposes. The New Testament says this quite clearly:

> *Jesus did many other miraculous signs in the presence of his disciples, which are not recorded in this book. But these are written that you may believe that Jesus is the Christ, the Son of God, and that by believing you may have life in his name. (John 20:30-31)*

> *Jesus did many other things as well. If every one of them were written down, I suppose that even the whole world would not have room for the books that would be written. (John 21:25)*

An example of something Jesus said that was never recorded is found in Acts 20:35 where Paul quoted a statement by Jesus that is nowhere found in the Gospels:

> *In everything I did, I showed you that by this kind of hard work we must help the weak, remembering the words the Lord Jesus himself said: "It is more blessed to give than to receive."*

The Old Testament also testifies to this same fact:

> *The secret things belong to the Lord our God, but the things revealed belong to us and to our children forever, that we may follow all the words of this law. (Deuteronomy 29:29)*

This fact should not concern us, however, since everything that is in the Bible is God's infallible Word. Furthermore, **everything that we need to know** is contained in God's Word.

God's purpose in giving us the Scripture was not to answer every question that our minds could possibly conceive, but God has revealed what needed to be revealed **that we may believe and obey Him!**

> *…the things revealed belong to us and to our children forever, that we may follow all the words of this law. (Deuteronomy 29:29)*

> *Do not add to what I command you and do not subtract from it, but keep the commands of the Lord your God that I give you. (Deuteronomy 4:2)*

> *But these are written that you may believe that Jesus is the Christ, the Son of God, and that by believing you may have life in his name. (John 20:31)*

So, the Bible, while entirely true and absolutely authoritative, is also selective. The Bible is given to us that we may know what God wants us to know and that we may obey Him, not so we can conjecture about what is not contained in it.

To speculate about things that are not clearly revealed in the Bible is foolish and will lead to deception.

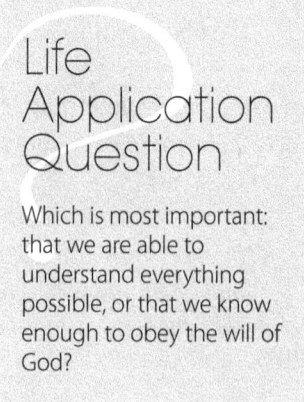

Life Application Question

Which is most important: that we are able to understand everything possible, or that we know enough to obey the will of God?

Stay with the Word! Many lives have been shipwrecked over the centuries when people departed from the clearly revealed Word of God and ventured into areas they shouldn't have. Let us have the heart of King David:

> *My heart is not proud, O Lord, my eyes are not haughty; I do not concern myself with great matters or things too wonderful for me. (Psalm 131:1)*

There is more than enough in the written Word of God for the greatest and most brilliant men and women to spend a lifetime learning and obeying it without venturing into areas God has left hidden.

> *To all perfection I see a limit; but your commands are boundless. (Psalm 119:96)*

Modern Prophetic Revelation

We are living in the days of the outpouring of the Holy Spirit, and one of the characteristics of these times is the restoration of the gift of prophecy, as well as the ministry of the prophet, to the Body of Christ.

> *And afterward, I will pour out my Spirit on all people. Your sons and daughters will prophesy, your old men will dream dreams, your young men will see visions. (Joel 2:28)*

It is a wonderful blessing that God is speaking through the gifts of the Holy Spirit to His people today, all around the world.

Yet, in the midst of this, we must remember that the Word of God stands as ultimately authoritative in all matters and in all circumstances. Everything that ever comes forth as a supernatural revelation must always be tested against the eternal standard of the Word of God. Isaiah wrote:

> *To the law and to the testimony! If they do not speak according to this word, they have no light of dawn. (Isaiah 8:20)*

No doctrine, teaching, practice, prophecy, dream or revelation should ever be accepted if it does not fully agree with the written Word of God. God has already given us His complete Word. Nothing will ever be added to it or taken away from it:

> *I warn everyone who hears the words of the prophecy of this book: If anyone adds anything to them, God will add to him the plagues described in this book. And if anyone takes words away from this book of prophecy, God will take away from him his share in the tree of life and in the holy city, which are described in this book. (Revelation 22:18-19)*

> *Do not add to what I command you and do not subtract from it, but keep the commands of the Lord your God that I give you. (Deuteronomy 4:2)*

This is so important because in these days we are not only experiencing an outpouring of the Holy Spirit, but we are also in the midst of increasing demonic activity on the earth. Jesus prophesied that this would happen in the last days:

> *At that time if anyone says to you, "Look, here is the Christ!" or, "There he is!" do not believe it. For false Christs and false prophets will appear and perform great signs and miracles to deceive even the elect – if that were possible. (Matthew 24:23-24)*

Paul also wrote:

> *The Spirit clearly says that in later times some will abandon the faith and follow deceiving spirits and things taught by demons. Such teachings come through hypocritical liars, whose consciences have been seared as with a hot iron. They forbid people to marry and order them to abstain from certain foods, which God created to be received with thanksgiving by those who believe and who know the truth. (1 Timothy 4:1-3)*

The only basis we have for evaluating doctrine and prophetic utterances is the written Word of God. Never believe anything that contradicts the Word! The Spirit of God will never declare anything that contradicts the written Word of God. If a spirit denies the Word then it is not the Holy Spirit but another spirit.

> *Dear friends, do not believe every spirit, but test the spirits to see whether they are from God, because many false prophets have gone out into the world. (1 John 4:1)*

We have a solemn duty to test what is presented to us as "Thus saith the Lord," and the sole standard by which we must test everything is the written Word of God. It does not matter how many "signs and wonders" may accompany it; if it does not line up with the written Word of God, then reject it!

> *But even if we or an angel from heaven should preach a gospel other than the one we preached to you, let him be eternally condemned! (Galatians 1:8)*

Paul said even if an angel from heaven gives you a revelation, if it doesn't agree with the Scriptures then refuse it.

Can you see why it is so important that we diligently learn the Word of God? If you do not know the Word, how will you be able to test that which is presented to you? Satan does not introduce himself as the deceiver that he is, but he comes as an "angel of light."

> *For such men are false apostles, deceitful workmen, masquerading as apostles of Christ. And no wonder, for Satan himself masquerades as an angel of light. (2 Corinthians 11:13-14)*

Life Application Question

If someone speaks a "prophetic word" to you that does not line up with the written Word of God, which should you obey: the "prophetic word" or the written Word?

God has promised to preserve us and to protect us from error and deception:

> *May God himself, the God of peace, sanctify you through and through. May your whole spirit, soul and body be kept blameless at the coming of our Lord Jesus Christ. The one who calls you is faithful and he will do it. (1 Thessalonians 5:23-24)*

Let us, therefore, draw near to Him through the Scriptures, diligently learning His Word and obeying it. If we will do that, we will not ultimately be deceived; He will keep us and present us before His throne on the Last Day, spotless and without blame.

Summary

1. Down through history God has watched over His Word initially to produce it and then to preserve and protect it.

2. The Bible we hold in our hands today is the complete and infallible Word of God.

3. The written Word of God is the ultimate standard of all truth.

4. All doctrines and prophetic utterances must agree with the written Word of God or we must reject them.

Review 4

1. How many books are there:

    In the Old Testament? _____

    In the New Testament? _____

    In the entire Bible? _____

2. Which Old Testament figure is probably responsible for fixing the Old Testament canon?

    ☐ Joseph
    ☐ Moses
    ☐ Ezra
    ☐ Paul

3. What is the Septuagint?

    ☐ A translation of the Old Testament Scriptures into Greek.
    ☐ A Jewish soft drink.
    ☐ False books that claimed to be God's Word.

4. What criteria were used to authenticate the Old Testament canon?

    ☐ The content of the books must be in harmony with the law.
    ☐ The books must have been written between Moses and Ezra.
    ☐ The language of the original books had to be Hebrew.
    ☐ They had to be written within the geographical boundaries of Israel.
    ☐ All of the above.
    ☐ None of the above.

5. What did the Jews mean by "The Law, the Prophets and the Writings"?

    ☐ Jewish traditions.
    ☐ Jewish mystical writings.
    ☐ The Old Testament.
    ☐ The New Testament.
    ☐ Only what Moses wrote.

6. Write out Matthew 5:18.

    _____

    _____

7. Please write "true" or "false" beside each of these statements:

    _____ To become a part of the canon, a New Testament book had to be written by an apostle or by a companion of an apostle.

    _____ The Apocrypha is part of the inspired Word of God.

    _____ Literature from the Early Church, such as the Apostolic Fathers, should not be considered as authoritative as the New Testament books.

    _____ The Pseudepigrapha are false documents.

    _____ Everything that God has ever revealed to man has been written in the Bible.

    _____ Everything we need to know has been written in the Bible.

    _____ It is good to know the Bible, whether we obey it or not.

    _____ God may give new revelation today, through vision or prophecy, that will contradict what is written in the Bible.

8. Complete these references:

   …If they do not speak according to _____ _____, they have no _____ of dawn. (Isaiah 8:20)

   But even if we or an _____ from _____ should preach a gospel other than the one we preached to you, let him be _____ _____! (Galatians 1:8)

9. If someone speaks a "prophetic word" to you that does not line up with the written Word of God, which should you obey: the "prophetic word" or the written Word? _____

The Ministry of the Word of God

The Word of God Is Alive

> *For the word of God is living and active.... (Hebrews 4:12)*

The Word of God is living and powerful.

> *And we also thank God continually because, when you received the word of God, which you heard from us, you accepted it not as the word of men, but as it actually is, the word of God, which is at work in you who believe. (1 Thessalonians 2:13)*

The Word of God "is at work" in those who believe. The Word of God has the power to change your life; it actually possesses the power to **do things** in your life.

We will now look at some of the specific things that the Word of God will do in your life as you "get into" the Word and the Word "gets into" you.

Faith

> *So then faith [cometh] by hearing, and hearing by the word of God. (Romans 10:17, KJV)*

We can see the divine order from this verse: the Word of God comes first, then "hearing," and then faith. In other words, the Word of God is first preached or taught, then the listener attends to that word with a desire to receive and obey it (i.e., he "hears" it), and then faith is produced in his heart.

There are three important things we can learn from this progression. Firstly, it must be the Word of God that is heard. The word of human tradition will not produce faith. Errors and heresy will not produce faith. It must be the Word of God.

Jesus told the religious leaders of His day that the Word of God, which should have been powerful in their lives, had been made ineffective by their human traditions:

> ...Thus you nullify the word of God for the sake of your tradition. (Matthew 15:6)

Secondly, there must be "hearing." The Word of God falling upon disinterested or disobedient ears will not produce faith. No matter how many books you read, tapes you hear, sermons you listen to, or meetings you attend, if you do not listen to the Word of God with a heart that is willing to receive and obey, faith will never grow in your heart. It will never happen.

This is one reason why so many Christians today are weak in faith. They spend so little time in the Word – and what time they do spend is usually hurried and haphazard – that faith never has the chance to grow. Furthermore, the word that is preached today is often so diluted with man's opinions, theories and misconceptions that even if you studied it night and day, it still would produce little faith.

Life Application Question

Will you automatically grow in faith simply by attending church meetings and just hearing the Word taught?

What response is necessary on your part?

Thirdly, when the Word is "heard" from an attentive and sincere heart, faith **will** come. As you diligently spend time in the Word of God and listen to anointed scriptural teaching, you will grow stronger in your faith. **It will work.** Your faith will grow.

Paul commended the Thessalonian Christians for their "faith (that was) growing more and more" (2 Thessalonians 1:3). This is because these believers had "received the word" and had diligently obeyed it (1 Thessalonians 1:6-10, KJV).

For your faith to grow continually, you must spend daily time in the Word, as well as time in the congregation of the saints, listening to the public preaching and teaching of the Word of God.

But, rest assured that your labors will not be in vain. The Word of God is alive and powerful, and as you do "hear" the Word with an attentive and obedient heart, faith will come.

The New Birth

> *He chose to give us birth through the word of truth, that we might be a kind of firstfruits of all he created. (James 1:18)*

> *For you have been born again, not of perishable seed, but of imperishable, through the living and enduring word of God. (1 Peter 1:23)*

The man who is born again has a new kind of life within him. It is life produced by the Word of God.

This life – this "seed" – will produce the fruits of life. In nature, the kind of fruit produced by the tree is determined by the kind of seed that produced the tree. An apple seed will produce an apple tree that will bear apples.

The divine seed of the Word of God in the heart of a believer will produce the divine nature in the life of that believer:

> *Through these he has given us his very great and precious promises, so that through them you may participate in the divine nature and escape the corruption in the world caused by evil desires. (2 Peter 1:4)*

When Peter says the Christian partakes of the "divine nature," he is not referring to God's "ontological" attributes (e.g., His deity, omnipresence, omniscience, omnipotence); rather, he is referring to the character attributes of God: His holiness, love, patience, purity, gentleness, etc.

The divine seed within us will bear divine fruit in our lives. Therefore, Paul speaks of the Christian bearing the "fruit of the Spirit":

> *But the fruit of the Spirit is love, joy, peace, patience, kindness, goodness, faithfulness, gentleness and self-control. Against such things there is no law. (Galatians 5:22-23)*

Furthermore, John writes that:

> *No one who is born of God will continue to sin, because God's seed remains in him; he cannot go on sinning, because he has been born of God. (1 John 3:9)*

This means that the born-again Christian who has divine life within him, through the implanted Word of God in his heart, will not continue in sin. God's Word, which is pure and holy, will produce fruit in your life that is pure and holy.

Before you were born again, you were the slave of sin, but now, you have life

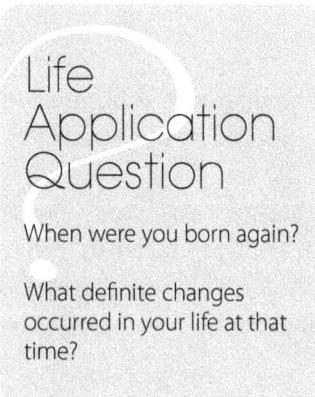

Life Application Question

When were you born again?

What definite changes occurred in your life at that time?

within you through the Word of God. And, as you yield to the Spirit and crucify the flesh, that life within you will produce victory, peace and righteousness in your life.

Spiritual Strength

> *The Spirit gives life; the flesh counts for nothing. The words I have spoken to you are spirit and they are life. (John 6:63)*
>
> *Jesus answered, "It is written: 'Man does not live on bread alone, but on every word that comes from the mouth of God.'" (Matthew 4:4)*
>
> *In fact, though by this time you ought to be teachers, you need someone to teach you the elementary truths of God's word all over again. You need milk, not solid food! (Hebrews 5:12)*

The idea of spiritual nourishment is contained in these verses. God's Word feeds and strengthens us spiritually. Just as our physical bodies need food and water to live, so we need God's Word for our very lives spiritually.

If you do not feed your body, what will happen? You will get sick, and eventually you will die. The fact that you had life once will not stop you from dying if you never feed yourself. You need physical food to maintain your physical life as well as to grow.

It is the same in the spiritual realm. Just as you were originally born again by the Word of God, so you need continual feeding by the Word of God to maintain your life and to grow.

We can read biographies of the great men and women of God who have lived over the years, and we may wish we could be like them. Well, the good news is that we can be like them! If we will do the same things they did, we will get the same results they got.

The great men and women of God down through history did many different things in their lives, but there was one thing that was constant for them all: **they were in the Word.**

It is said that George Müller read the Bible through several times each year. That is why he had such great faith. Smith Wigglesworth constantly read the Bible, and it was the only book he ever read in his life!

If you want to be spiritually strong, you must feed yourself spiritual food; you must do it regularly with the right kind of food.

In several places in the New Testament, the Word of God is described using different food analogies. We can use each of these analogies to describe a different stage of development in the life of the believer:

> *Like newborn babies, crave pure spiritual milk, so that by it you may grow up in your salvation,* (1 Peter 2:2)

> **Life Application Point**
>
> The Word of God makes us strong and healthy. Make a decision now to spend quality time *every* day in the Word of God.

Newborn babies drink milk. They do not eat meat since they are not able to chew it or to digest it.

> *Jesus answered, "It is written: 'Man does not live on bread alone, but on every word that comes from the mouth of God.'"* (Matthew 4:4)

In infancy, a child will begin to eat things like bread. This is more substantial than milk, but it is still not solid meat.

> *In fact, though by this time you ought to be teachers, you need someone to*

> **Life Application Question**
>
> Are you satisfied with your present level of maturity in the Word of God?
>
> What specific steps can you take to grow in this area of your life?

> *teach you the elementary truths of God's word all over again. You need milk, not solid food! Anyone who lives on milk, being still an infant, is not acquainted with the teaching about righteousness. But solid food is for the mature, who by constant use have trained themselves to distinguish good from evil. (Hebrews 5:12-14)*

As a child grows into his youth and then into adulthood, he begins to eat solid food and meat. An adult would not be satisfied with just milk. He needs more to maintain his strength and to grow. This is why many Christians are not satisfied in their churches today – because the Word that is taught is elementary and basic.

On the other hand, you should not give a baby meat to eat. It will choke him. We need to be sensitive to the maturity level of new Christians when we minister to them.

There are stages of development in the spiritual life, and we should not bypass any of them.

God's desire for His people is that we grow in maturity, and for that reason, He has given us His Word.

> *Now I commit you to God and to the word of his grace, which can build you up and give you an inheritance among all those who are sanctified. (Acts 20:32)*

The only habits we develop are the habits that we develop! So, let us be diligent in the Word of God in our lives, and let us encourage new Christians to cultivate diligence in the Scriptures.

Physical Healing

Several Scriptures teach us specifically that there is power to heal in the Word of God:

He sent forth his word and healed them; he rescued them from the grave. (Psalm 107:20)

My son, pay attention to what I say; listen closely to my words. Do not let them out of your sight, keep them within your heart; for they are life to those who find them and health to a man's whole body. (Proverbs 4:20-22)

The Word of God is "health" (not just healing) to "all" our flesh (not just certain parts). Hallelujah! What a promise! There is power in the Word of God to heal us from every kind of sickness and disease, and then to maintain us in health.

However, this does not happen automatically just because you are a Christian. Proverbs 4 teaches that we must "pay attention" to God's words and "listen closely" to His sayings. We must not let them "out of our sight"; rather we must keep them "within our hearts."

> **Life Application Question**
>
> If the Word of God promises healing and victory, why do you think so many Christians live in sickness and defeat?

This implies great diligence and obedience on our part in order to reap the consistent healing benefits of God's Word.

Jesus often healed with His Word:

…But just say the word, and my servant will be healed. (Matthew 8:8)

Then he said to the man, "Stretch out your hand." So he stretched it out and it was completely restored, just as sound as the other. (Matthew 12:13)

But that you may know that the Son of Man has authority on earth to forgive sins…" He said to the paralytic, "I tell you, get up, take your

> *mat and go home." He got up, took his mat and walked out in full view of them all.... (Mark 2:10-12)*

Indeed Jesus raised Lazarus from the dead with His Word:

> *When he had said this, Jesus called in a loud voice, "Lazarus, come out!" The dead man came out... (John 11:43-44)*

There is healing power in the Word of God. The power of medical science is limited, but God's Word is unlimited. Medicine cannot cure certain diseases, but God's Word knows no boundaries. Medicine may cure one part of your body while harming another, but God's Word is entirely effective. God's Word is unconditionally good for you – spirit, soul, mind and body. Avail yourself of it!

Deliverance

Just as God's Word has the power to heal our bodies, so it has the power to set us free from demonic oppression. This oppression may be spiritual or physical, and God's Word is the cure for both kinds.

Look at how Jesus set people free from demonic oppression:

> *When evening came, many who were demon-possessed were brought to him, and he drove out the spirits with a word and healed all the sick. (Matthew 8:16)*

In another place, a woman brought her oppressed daughter to Jesus, and Jesus referred to deliverance as "the children's bread" (Matthew 15:26). He then spoke the word of freedom for the daughter, and she was "healed from that very

> **Life Application Point**
>
> The Word of God gives us authority over Satan. That is why Satan works so hard to keep Christians out of the Word! He knows that if he can keep us from knowing and obeying the Word of God, he will defeat us.

hour" (v. 28). Deliverance is not something we need to beg or plead with God for. He has already provided it for us as "the children's bread," and His method of giving it to us is "with His word."

Jesus spoke the Word of God to defeat the devil in His wilderness temptations, and we can defeat the enemy the same way.

Wisdom and Understanding

The Word of God gives us wisdom and understanding:

> *The unfolding of your words gives light; it gives understanding to the simple. (Psalm 119:130)*

When I was saved, I owned many books. Starting from when I was about 12 years old, I was searching for truth. I had collected volumes on philosophy, psychology, the occult, the great works of literature and the writings of many religions (other than Christianity). I was searching for truth.

But, when I was saved, I discovered that one Book contains all that man could ever need. The Word of God is absolute truth. It is the final word on every subject. It is absolutely reliable and infallible. It contains everything that man needs for spiritual wisdom and understanding. When I discovered that, I got rid of all those other books and devoured the Bible.

> *For the wisdom of this world is foolishness in God's sight.... (1 Corinthians 3:19)*

Life Application Point

With all the brilliant achievements of modern technology, man is no closer to peace, happiness or true knowledge. But, the Word of God is our infallible, endless source of wisdom and understanding.

All the spiritual wisdom and knowledge we could ever possibly need are in the Word of God. Surely the Word of God should have first place in our lives!

One of the kinds of wisdom we can receive from God's Word is a revelation of His will for our lives. So many Christians live their lives in ignorance of what God's purposes for them are. Yet, we do not need to be ignorant because God's will is clearly revealed in His Word:

> *All Scripture is God-breathed and is useful for teaching, rebuking, correcting and training in righteousness, so that the man of God may be thoroughly equipped for every good work. (2 Timothy 3:16-17)*

The more we know the Word of God, the more we will understand His will for our lives.

The answers for all of life's questions will be in God's Word in either one of two ways:

1. **Specifically.** The issue itself you are asking about may be directly addressed in the Bible with God's will clearly revealed. For example, sexual immorality is specifically dealt with many times in the Bible:

> **Life Application Point**
>
> Many Christians ask others what God wants them to do when they should instead spend their time in God's Word. That's where the answers are!

> *It is God's will that you should be sanctified: that you should avoid sexual immorality; that each of you should learn to control his own body in a way that is holy and honorable, (1 Thessalonians 4:3-4)*

There is no doubt about whether or not fornication is permissible for a Christian! Likewise, many other issues are specifically addressed in the Bible.

2. **In principle.** Some issues are not directly addressed in the Scriptures. Consequently, in prayer, we should take the principles that are taught in the whole counsel of God and apply them to our specific situation. In this regard, there are certain passages that apply very well to a whole range of questions. For example, Paul's statement in 1 Corinthians 6:19-20 would keep a Christian from smoking, even though smoking is not specifically prohibited in the Bible:

> *Do you not know that your body is a temple of the Holy Spirit, who is in you, whom you have received from God? You are not your own; you were bought at a price. Therefore honor God with your body.*

Furthermore, there are broad principles taught in the Bible that can readily be applied to a large range of circumstances. For example:

> **Life Application Question**
>
> Often people who are trying to excuse their sin will say, "Well, it's not specifically forbidden in the Bible." Why is this dishonest?

> *So whether you eat or drink or whatever you do, do it all for the glory of God. (1 Corinthians 10:31)*

> *And whatever you do, whether in word or deed, do it all in the name of the Lord Jesus, giving thanks to God the Father through him. (Colossians 3:17)*

The principles taught in these verses, especially when bathed in prayer, will be sufficient to give a clear understanding of what God's will is concerning many issues that are not otherwise dealt with in the Scriptures.

> **Life Application Point**
>
> Feeling sorry for ourselves when we fail will not make us strong. Spending time in God's Word will. If you have failed in an area, get back up on your feet, dust yourself off, and get back into the Word! That is where your life and strength are found.

Victory Over Sin

The Word of God has great power to keep us from sin. Consider the words of King David:

> *I have hidden your word in my heart that I might not sin against you. (Psalm 119:11)*

> *As for the deeds of men – by the word of your lips I have kept myself from the ways of the violent. (Psalm 17:4)*

The Word of God reveals God's will to us concerning all kinds of specific activities, and so, it keeps us from sin. Furthermore, while certain things are not expressly named in the Bible, we are still given the general principle of Colossians 3:17:

> *And whatever you do, whether in word or deed, do it all in the name of the Lord Jesus, giving thanks to God the Father through him.*

Thus, through the revelation of God's Word to our hearts, we are kept from all kinds of sin.

Moreover, the Word of God keeps us from sin by its inherent power. As we grow strong spiritually through the Word, we will have the spiritual energy to resist the temptations the enemy sends our way. The more solid our convictions are, based upon the Word of God, the stronger will be our power to resist temptation, as well as to withstand the winds of trial, tribulation and adversity that the Lord allows us to experience.

Victory Over Satan

The Word of God is not only effective in our personal war against sin; it is also powerful against the devil. Jesus defeated the devil through quoting the Word of God in His wilderness testing. For example:

Jesus answered, "It is written: 'Worship the Lord your God and serve him only.'" (Luke 4:8)

In his list of our spiritual weapons, Paul told us to take "the sword of the Spirit, which is the word of God" (Ephesians 6:17). All the other items that Paul named in Ephesians 6 – the girdle, the breastplate, the shoes, the shield and the helmet – are defensive components of our armor. The sword is the only offensive piece that Paul speaks of, and it is the Word of God.

> **Life Application Question**
>
> What are some areas of your life in which you have effectively used the Word of God as a weapon? What are some areas in which you could do it better?

In order to be effective in spiritual warfare, we must know the Word of God, we must obey it, and then we must use it. It is not enough just to know the Word; we must also put it to work.

…I write to you, young men, because you are strong, and the word of God lives in you, and you have overcome the evil one. (1 John 2:14)

The young Christians of John's day had been successful in their fight against the devil because the Word of God was abiding in them. They knew God, they knew His Word, and they used His Word to defeat their spiritual adversary.

They overcame him by the blood of the Lamb and by the word of their testimony; they did not love their lives so much as to shrink from death. (Revelation 12:11)

The Word of God on the lips of a surrendered, blood-washed believer is sufficient to put the hosts of the enemy to flight.

Cleansing

Several Scriptures speak of the cleansing power of God's Word:

> *You are already clean because of the word I have spoken to you. (John 15:3)*

> *...Christ loved the church and gave himself up for her to make her holy, cleansing her by the washing with water through the word, and to present her to himself as a radiant church, without stain or wrinkle or any other blemish, but holy and blameless. (Ephesians 5:25-27)*

These are a number of ways that God's Word cleanses us:

> **Life Application Point**
>
> In this world, we often are exposed to the filth of sin. That is why we must continually experience the cleansing, purifying power of God's Word.

1. In the new birth, God's Word, along with Jesus' blood, cleanses us from our sin.

2. In our daily lives, we are soiled by our contact through the world. Nevertheless, when we come apart to God and spend time in His Word, it cleans our spirits and our minds.

3. As we grow in God through His Word, He reveals more and more of our hearts to us. What was hidden before becomes manifest. Then, by the power of His Word, He changes us and transforms us into Jesus' image.

> *Do not conform any longer to the pattern of this world, but be transformed by the renewing of your mind. Then you will be able to test and approve what God's will is – his good, pleasing and perfect will. (Romans 12:2)*

When God is done with us, we will be a glorious church, "without stain or wrinkle or any other blemish."

Peter speaks of the power of the Word of God to cleanse and mature us:

> *Through these he has given us his very great and precious promises, so that through them you may participate in the divine nature and escape the corruption in the world caused by evil desires. (2 Peter 1:4)*

It is by the promises of God, which are revealed in His Word, that we are cleansed from the corruption of the world, and then, we increasingly "participate in the divine nature."

Revelation

The Bible speaks of itself as being a "mirror" in several different ways:

> *Anyone who listens to the word but does not do what it says is like a man who looks at his face in a mirror and, after looking at himself, goes away and immediately forgets what he looks like. But the man who looks intently into the perfect law that gives freedom, and continues to do this, not forgetting what he has heard, but doing it – he will be blessed in what he does. (James 1:23-25)*

As we read the Word of God, it reveals to us what we really look like to God. As a physical mirror reveals the appearance of our outward, physical man to us, so the Word of God reveals the reality of our inward, spiritual man to us. It is then up to us to respond to this revelation and not to ignore it. If we ignore the revelation, we will never be changed. On the other hand, if we respond to God

Life Application Point

As we fellowship with Jesus through His Word, we encounter His life-giving, lifechanging power.

with yielded hearts, then the Word becomes liberty and life to us, and we shall be changed and blessed.

Paul also spoke of the Word as a mirror in 2 Corinthians 3:18:

> *And we, who with unveiled faces all reflect the Lord's glory, are being transformed into his likeness with ever-increasing glory, which comes from the Lord, who is the Spirit.*

Here the mirror of God's Word reveals to us, not our sins, but the Lord Jesus Christ; not what we are in ourselves, but what we are in Him; not our faults and failings, but the glory of the Lord. Paul says it is while we look into this mirror that we are transformed into that same image.

This is the power of the Word of God. It contains within itself the power to change our lives from head to toe. This is the secret of God's transforming grace in our lives. As we abide in His Word and His Word abides in us, we will become more and more like Him who birthed us in His own image.

The Word and the Spirit

The Holy Spirit breathed out the Word of God originally. One of His titles is "the Spirit of Truth" (John 16:13). The Word of God is also called the "sword of the Spirit" (Ephesians 6:17). So we need the ministry of the Holy Spirit in our lives in two special ways that relate to His Word:

1. The Word must be revealed to us by the Spirit, and not by our own intellect or human wisdom.

   > *The man without the Spirit does not accept the things*

> **Life Application Point**
>
> So many churches go to one extreme or the other; they are either strong in the Word and weak in the Spirit, or strong in the Spirit and weak in the Word. But the Christian should be balanced and strong in both.

> *that come from the Spirit of God, for they are foolishness to him, and he cannot understand them, because they are spiritually discerned. (1 Corinthians 2:14)*

The Holy Spirit is the perfect Interpreter of the Scriptures to us. That is one reason why God gave Him to the church: to quicken and reveal His Word.

> *But when he, the Spirit of truth, comes, he will guide you into all truth. He will not speak on his own; he will speak only what he hears, and he will tell you what is yet to come. (John 16:13)*

> *but God has revealed it to us by his Spirit. The Spirit searches all things, even the deep things of God. For who among men knows the thoughts of a man except the man's spirit within him? In the same way no one knows the thoughts of God except the Spirit of God. We have not received the spirit of the world but the Spirit who is from God, that we may understand what God has freely given us. (1 Corinthians 2:10-12)*

2. The Word must be ministered with the Spirit. When we minister the Word of God to others, we must do it by the Spirit.

    > *This is what we speak, not in words taught us by human wisdom but in words taught by the Spirit, expressing spiritual truths in spiritual words. (1 Corinthians 2:13)*

    > *But you will receive power when the Holy Spirit comes on you; and you will be my witnesses... (Acts 1:8)*

    It is only as we learn to be able ministers of the Spirit of God, as well as of His Word, that our preaching and teaching will:

    A. Be accurate. The Holy Spirit reveals the Word that He inspired.

B. Be effective. The Holy Spirit empowers the ministry of the Word.

C. Reveal His character as well as His law. We must be able to minister life to others as well as conviction.

Summary

1. The Word of God is living and powerful. It changes our lives.

2. Specifically, the Word of God produces:
    a) Faith.
    b) The new birth.
    c) Spiritual strength.
    d) Physical healing.
    e) Deliverance.
    f) Wisdom and understanding.
    g) Victory over sin.
    h) Victory over Satan.
    i) Cleansing.
    j) Revelation and transformation.

3. The Holy Spirit breathed out the Word of God originally. Therefore, we need the Spirit's ministry to:
    a) Properly understand the Word ourselves.
    b) Effectively minister the Word to others.

Review 5

1. The Word of God:

   ☐ Is living.
   ☐ Is powerful.
   ☐ Has the power to change your life.
   ☐ All of the above.
   ☐ None of the above.

2. Mark the three things that we can learn from Romans 10:17:

   ☐ Faith comes by praying for it.
   ☐ It is only the Word of God that produces faith.
   ☐ Faith comes through passively listening to sermons.
   ☐ For faith to grow in your heart, you must listen to the Word of God with a heart that is willing to receive and obey.
   ☐ Faith is a great mystery. We really do not know how it comes.
   ☐ When the Word is "heard" from an attentive and sincere heart, faith will come.

3. Please write "true" or "false" beside each of these statements, and give a Scripture reference to support your answer:

   _____ We are born again through the Word of God.
   Scripture: _____

   _____ We need the Word of God for spiritual strength.
   Scripture: _____

   _____ Those who are young in the Lord should be fed the "milk" of the Word and not the "meat" of the Word.
   Scripture: _____

_____ There is power to heal in the Word of God.
Scripture: _____

_____ The Word of God has the power to set us free from demonic oppression.
Scripture: _____

_____ The Word of God gives us wisdom and understanding.
Scripture: _____

_____ God is impressed with the wisdom of this world.
Scripture: _____

_____ Even issues that aren't explicitly addressed in the Bible are still addressed in principle.
Scripture: _____

_____ The Word of God has the power to keep us from sin.
Scripture: _____

_____ The Word of God will always defeat the devil.
Scripture: _____

_____ The Word of God will cleanse us from sin.
Scripture: _____

_____ When we obediently look into the mirror of the Word of God we will be transformed into Jesus' image.
Scripture: _____

_____ The Word must be revealed to us by the Spirit, and not by our own intellect or human wisdom.
Scripture: _____

_____ The Word must be ministered to others with the Spirit.
Scripture: _____

The Basic Doctrines

Therefore let us leave the elementary teachings about Christ and go on to maturity, not laying again the foundation of repentance from acts that lead to death, and of faith in God, instruction about baptisms, the laying on of hands, the resurrection of the dead, and eternal judgment. (Hebrews 6:1-2)

Paul, in these two verses, defines what are the "elementary teachings about Christ." They are also called "the foundation." These are the basic doctrines of the Christian faith. They are "foundational" doctrines. Before we can build, we must first have the foundation laid properly.

It is interesting to note that Paul's first foundational doctrine is repentance which is the start of the Christian's new life in Christ, and the last foundational doctrine is eternal judgment. Thus, the entire length of the Christian's life is covered – from time into eternity.

Life Application Question

Many Christians study advanced things in God yet have not mastered the basics. Do you think this is right?

Why not?

There are six foundational doctrines named here:

1. Repentance from dead works.
2. Faith in God.
3. Instruction about baptisms.
4. Laying on of hands.
5. Resurrection of the dead.
6. Eternal judgment.

We will now look at each of these doctrines in order.

Review 6

1. Please write out the six foundational doctrines named in Hebrews 6:1-2:

    a) _____

    b) _____

    c) _____

    d) _____

    e) _____

    f) _____

Repentance From Dead Works

Repentance is not a popular subject, but it is central to the Christian life. The Bible teaches that repentance precedes forgiveness of sins:

> *Peter replied, "Repent and be baptized, every one of you, in the name of Jesus Christ for the forgiveness of your sins. And you will receive the gift of the Holy Spirit." (Acts 2:38)*

Jesus said that without repentance man will perish in his sins:

> *…But unless you repent, you too will all perish. (Luke 13:3)*

The Meaning of Repentance

1. In the Old Testament, two words are translated "repent":

   a) To be sorry. For example:

   > *And it repented the Lord that he had made man on the earth, and it grieved him at his heart. (Genesis 6:6, KJV)*

   God did not "repent" in the same way a sinner "repents." Instead, He "regretted" that He had made man. He was grieved.

b) To turn. For example:

> *Therefore say to the house of Israel, "This is what the Sovereign Lord says: Repent! Turn from your idols and renounce all your detestable practices!" (Ezekiel 14:6)*

2. In the New Testament, to repent means to change one's mind. For example:

> *Repent, then, and turn to God, so that your sins may be wiped out, that times of refreshing may come from the Lord, (Acts 3:19)*

So, the following definition harmonizes the meanings of the word in both testaments: to "repent" means to regret your way of life, to change your mind about it and to turn away from it and towards God.

For the sinner to "repent" means that he makes an inward decision to turn the course of his life from dead works to serve God:

> *for they themselves report what kind of reception you gave us. They tell how you turned to God from idols to serve the living and true God, (1 Thessalonians 1:9)*

The True Gospel Always Includes the Preaching of Repentance

John the Baptist was Jesus' forerunner, and he preached repentance:

> *It is written in Isaiah the prophet: "I will send my messenger ahead of you, who will prepare your way"…And so John came, baptizing in the desert region and preaching a baptism of repentance for the forgiveness of sins. (Mark 1:2-4)*

Jesus preached repentance:

> *After John was put in prison, Jesus went into Galilee, proclaiming the good news of God. "The time has come," he said. "The kingdom of God is near. Repent and believe the good news!" (Mark 1:14-15)*

Jesus' disciples preached repentance:

> *They went out and preached that people should repent. (Mark 6:12)*

> *He told them, "This is what is written: The Christ will suffer and rise from the dead on the third day, and repentance and forgiveness of sins will be preached in his name to all nations, beginning at Jerusalem." (Luke 24:46-47)*

Paul's message was one of repentance:

> *You know that I have not hesitated to preach anything that would be helpful to you but have taught you publicly and from house to house. I have declared to both Jews and Greeks that they must turn to God in repentance and have faith in our Lord Jesus. (Acts 20:20-21)*

God, Himself, "commands all people everywhere to repent" (Acts 17:30)! Without true repentance, any profession of faith will be empty words. Any gospel that leaves out repentance is a false gospel. Any "faith message" that does not equally stress repentance will never work.

> **Life Application Question**
>
> To preach repentance will often make you unpopular. Would it be wise to tone down the truth to become more acceptable to men?

Repentance Is More Than Feeling Sorry

A common misconception about repentance is that it is primarily an emotion. Repentance does involve regret because if you do not regret your sinful way of life with its consequences of death and alienation from God, you will never truly turn from it. However, repentance is more than regret. Repentance is an inward decision to change which results in outward actions of change.

After he betrayed Jesus, Judas **regretted** his sin:

> When Judas, who had betrayed him, saw that Jesus was condemned, he was seized with remorse and returned the thirty silver coins to the chief priests and the elders. (Matthew 27:3)

Nevertheless, Judas did not truly **repent**, and he was lost eternally:

> ... this apostolic ministry, which Judas left to go where he belongs. (Acts 1:25)

> **Life Application Question**
>
> Can you remember times in your life when you experienced an emotion of sorrow over sin, and yet, you did not experience lasting change?

It is possible for people to shed tears when they are under conviction of sin, when they are caught in their sin, or when they receive the bad consequences of their sin, but never actually to change their mind about their life and receive salvation. True repentance involves change. Repentance is not primarily an emotion but a decision: a decision to turn from sin to serve Jesus.

Paul spoke of the relationship of "godly sorrow" to true repentance in 2 Corinthians 7:10, and the difference between that and false "worldly sorrow":

Godly sorrow brings repentance that leads to salvation and leaves no regret, but worldly sorrow brings death. (2 Corinthians 7:10)

True Repentance Will Result in Works of Righteousness

Repentance is an inward decision that produces outward change. Without the outward change there is doubt the inward decision was ever real.

John the Baptist told those coming to him for baptism to, "Produce fruit in keeping with repentance" (Matthew 3:8). In other words, John told them first to prove that they had repented by their good works, and then come to his baptism. Outward works prove the genuineness of inward repentance.

Paul preached the same kind of repentance – a repentance that is not just words but one that results in works:

> *First to those in Damascus, then to those in Jerusalem and in all Judea, and to the Gentiles also, I preached that they should repent and turn to God and prove their repentance by their deeds. (Acts 26:20)*

Life Application Point

Outward works are not just outward words. *Words* can be spoken easily, but our *works* show the reality of what happened in our hearts.

A Picture of Repentance

The parable of the prodigal son is a wonderful picture of repentance. Read Luke 15:11-32.

After the son had wasted all his substance and been reduced to the humiliation of the "pig pen," he made a quality, inward decision to turn in a different direction:

> *I will set out and go back to my father and say to him: Father, I have sinned against heaven and against you. (Luke 15:18)*

That inward decision then resulted in outward action:

> *So he got up and went to his father... (Luke 15:20)*

And his father responded graciously to his true repentance:

> *...But while he was still a long way off, his father saw him and was filled with compassion for him; he ran to his son, threw his arms around him and kissed him. (Luke 15:20)*

This is a wonderful picture of the sinner's true repentance and turning to God, and God's resulting acceptance of him!

Repentance Is a Gift from God

The Scripture teaches that repentance is a gift of God:

> *Restore us to yourself, O Lord, that we may return;... (Lamentations 5:21)*

> *God exalted him to his own right hand as Prince and Savior that he might give repentance and forgiveness of sins to Israel. (Acts 5:31)*

> *..."So then, God has granted even the Gentiles repentance unto life." (Acts 11:18)*

Life Application Question

Have you ever stopped and thanked God for giving you the gift of repentance?

Also, when you pray for others, do you pray that God will "give them repentance"?

> *And the Lord's servant must not quarrel; instead, he must be kind to everyone, able to teach, not resentful. Those who oppose him he must gently instruct, in the hope that God will grant them repentance leading them to a knowledge of the truth, (2 Timothy 2:24-25)*

From your side, however, you should not wait until you feel that God has given you the gift of repentance, but you should repent as soon as you see the need to do so. From your side, there is nothing stopping you from repenting. The Scripture teaches that "**now** is the time of God's favor, **now** is the day of salvation" (2 Corinthians 6:2).

Esau and Repentance

At this point, it would be profitable to examine a verse about Esau that is sometimes misquoted in this regard.

> *For ye know how that afterward, when he would have inherited the blessing, he was rejected: for he found no place of repentance, though he sought it carefully with tears. (Hebrews 12:17, KJV)*

In a careless moment, Esau sold his birthright to his brother Jacob in exchange for a bowl of soup. But later he regretted what he had done, and he went to his father Isaac and with tears tried to obtain the blessing that was once his:

> *Esau said to his father, "Do you have only one blessing, my father? Bless me too, my father!" Then Esau wept aloud. (Genesis 27:38)*

The repentance (or change of mind) that Esau sought was not his own but his father's. He wanted his father to change his mind and take the blessing from Jacob and give it back to him. However, Isaac would not change his mind.

> *Isaac trembled violently and said, "Who was it, then, that hunted game and brought it to me? I ate it just before you came and I blessed him – and indeed he will be blessed!" (Genesis 27:33)*

Isaac had already given the blessing, and he could not take it back from Jacob.

In this way, Esau "found no place of repentance, though he sought it carefully with tears."

If you do not understand the meaning of this, you may have the picture of Esau trying to repent of his sin but not being able to because God was withholding the gift of repentance from him. However, that is not the case. The repentance (or change of mind) that Esau sought with tears was not his own but his father's.

Although repentance is a gift from God's side, from your side there is nothing stopping you from repenting right now if you need to. So, do not let a misconception about this verse stop you from forsaking sin and coming to God on the basis that you do not think God has given you or even wants to give you the gift of repentance. God is not holding back repentance from you. If you do not repent, it is because you choose not to repent; it is not because God denied you something you wanted.

> **Life Application Point**
>
> You are responsible for what you do, and you will be judged one day for your actions. Never let any doctrine rob you of your sense of responsibility before God.

Remember:

> *(God) commands all people everywhere to repent. (Acts 17:30)*

That means you are responsible to repent and to get right with God. After you do repent you will look back and realize that God gave you repentance, but at the time, you were only doing what you chose to do.

Summary

1. Without repentance, there is no forgiveness of sins. Repentance is central to the Gospel.

2. To "repent" means to regret your way of life, to change your mind about it and to turn away from it and toward God.

3. Repentance is more than just feeling sorry; it is an inward decision to change that results in outward actions of change.

4. True repentance will result in works of righteousness.

5. Repentance is a gift from God, while from your side you are responsible to repent now.

Review 7

1. In the Old Testament "repentance" can mean:

   ☐ To be sorry.
   ☐ To turn.
   ☐ It can mean either, depending on the original word used.

2. In the New Testament, to "repent" means:

   ☐ To change one's church.
   ☐ To change one's clothes.
   ☐ To change one's mind.
   ☐ To change the way one speaks.

3. Complete this sentence:

   To "repent" means to _____ your way of _____, to _____ your _____ about it and to _____ away from it and towards _____.

4. The true Gospel will include the preaching of repentance:

   ☐ Always.
   ☐ Never.
   ☐ Sometimes.
   ☐ Depends on the situation.

5. Who told people to repent in the New Testament?

    ☐ John the Baptist.
    ☐ Jesus.
    ☐ Jesus' disciples.
    ☐ Paul.
    ☐ God Himself.
    ☐ All of the above.
    ☐ None of the above.

6. Complete this sentence:

    Repentance is _____ than just feeling sorry: it is an inward _____ to _____ that results in outward _____ of change.

7. True repentance will result in works of righteousness:

    ☐ Sometimes.
    ☐ Always.

8. Please write "true" or "false" beside each of these statements, and give a Scripture reference to support your answer:

    _____ Repentance is a gift of God.
    Scripture: _____

    _____ God does not expect you to repent unless you feel like it emotionally.
    Scripture: _____

Faith Toward God

And without faith it is impossible to please God, because anyone who comes to him must believe that he exists and that he rewards those who earnestly seek him. (Hebrews 11:6)

...everything that does not come from faith is sin. (Romans 14:23)

Faith is central to the life of a Christian. Faith is necessary to please God. Without faith, we will not even come to Him. Without faith, nothing in our lives will be acceptable to God. We may perform many religious acts, but without faith, none of it will please God; our whole life will be "sin" in His eyes. Faith is so important that in several places in the New Testament Christianity is called "the faith" (e.g., Jude 3; Galatians 1:23). But what is faith?

Faith is one of the few terms specifically defined in the Bible:

Now faith is the substance of things hoped for, the evidence of things not seen. (Hebrews 11:1, KJV)

This verse shows us that faith is different from hope. Hope is an expectancy concerning things in the future, whereas faith is a "substance," based upon our future hope that we possess now.

True faith is in the heart:

For it is with your heart that you believe and are justified... (Romans 10:10)

It is more than merely agreeing with truth. It involves a heart receiving and submitting to that truth.

Faith Is Not Mental Assent

Since faith is in the heart, it is important to understand the profound difference between faith and mental assent. Many Christians theoretically "believe" in Jesus. They agree with the doctrines of the Bible. Intellectually they concur with the truths of Christianity, but their "head faith" produces no change in their lives.

Faith, on the other hand, has "substance" – spiritual dynamic and reality – to it. It will change your life from head to toe, and it will give you assurance right now. If your Christianity is merely "head faith," you will not possess assurance of your salvation or of any of the other promises of God. Faith has spiritual "substance"; it is not just mentally agreeing with the doctrines of the Bible.

> **Life Application Point**
>
> This is one of the major deficiencies of modern Western Christianity: a confusion of mental assent with real heart faith.

Faith Is Not Sight

> *We live by faith, not by sight. (2 Corinthians 5:7)*

Paul contrasts faith and sight in this verse. To "live by sight" means that your life is dominated and controlled by what you see and feel in the natural world around you.

To live by faith, on the other hand, means that you live according to the written Word of God.

If we live by sight, we will live according to only what our natural senses tell us, but if we live by faith in God, we will put His Word as a higher authority than what we see and feel. To the spiritual man, sight comes after faith, not before it. Consider the words of David:

> *[I had fainted], unless I had believed to see the goodness of the Lord in the land of the living. (Psalm 27:13, KJV)*

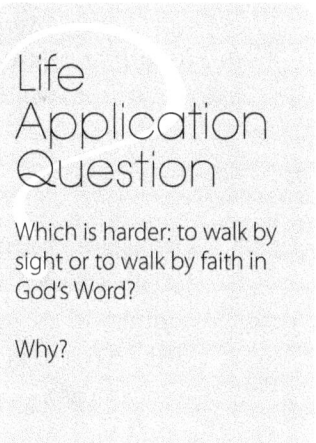

Life Application Question

Which is harder: to walk by sight or to walk by faith in God's Word?

Why?

In the midst of very difficult circumstances, David believed the promises of God rather than being overwhelmed by his apparently hopeless situation. Because of his faith, his circumstances later changed, but his faith came first: he "believed to see."

Jesus taught that faith comes first, and sight comes second:

> *Then Jesus said, "Did I not tell you that if you believed, you would see the glory of God?" (John 11:40)*

If you can already see a thing, you do not need faith to believe it. You need faith to believe what you cannot see or feel. Many immature Christians only believe what they see, but the mature Christian will see what he believes (when he believes the Word of God).

There are a number of examples in the Bible of men and women who chose to walk by faith in the Word of God rather than according to the evidence of their feelings or circumstances.

ABRAHAM:

> *As it is written: "I have made you a father of many nations." He is our father in the sight of God, in whom he believed – the God who gives life to the dead and **calls things that are not as though they***

> *were. Against all hope, Abraham in hope believed and so became the father of many nations, just as it had been said to him, "So shall your offspring be."* **Without weakening in his faith, he faced the fact that his body was as good as dead** *– since he was about a hundred years old – and that Sarah's womb was also dead. Yet he did not waver through unbelief regarding the promise of God, but* **was strengthened in his faith** *and gave glory to God, being fully persuaded that God had power to do what he had promised. (Romans 4:17-21)*

Abraham did 3 things:

1. He believed the promise of God that he would have a son.
2. He disregarded the physical evidence before him that was contrary to the promise of God.
3. He held fast to his faith, and in the end saw the promise of God come to pass.

MARY:

> *"How will this be," Mary asked the angel, "since I am a virgin?" The angel answered, "The Holy Spirit will come upon you, and the power of the Most High will overshadow you. So the holy one to be born will be called the Son of God. Even Elizabeth your relative is going to have a child in her old age, and she who was said to be barren is in her sixth month. For nothing is impossible with God." "I am the Lord's servant," Mary answered.* **"May it be to me as you have said."** *Then the angel left her. (Luke 1:34-38)*

Mary believed the Word of God despite the impossibility of the promise. For that reason, God commended her by His Spirit in Elizabeth:

> *Blessed is she who has believed that what the Lord has said to her will be accomplished! (Luke 1:45)*

You too will be commended by God when you believe the promises of His Word in the face of impossible circumstances.

PETER:
> *When he had finished speaking, he said to Simon, "Put out into deep water, and let down the nets for a catch." Simon answered, "Master, we've worked hard all night and haven't caught anything. But because you say so, I will let down the nets." When they had done so, they caught such a large number of fish that their nets began to break. (Luke 5:4-6)*

In spite of the apparent foolishness of Jesus' instructions, Peter believed His word and let down the net. Look at the result!

The Difference Between Faith and Presumption

We must point out that the kind of faith that works is only **faith in God** based upon His Word. "Faith" will not work when it is not based upon God's promise. Furthermore, even faith in God's promises will not work when the conditions for receiving those promises are not met.

Moreover, a living faith in God is born out of a living relationship with Him. Faith is not really faith at all unless it is the spontaneous consequence of a personal relationship with the Faithful One; not out of guilt nor constraint nor perceived religious duty but simply the natural result of a sincere fellowship of love with God.

We will only really trust one whom we know. Those who **know** God will put their trust in Him.

> *Those who know your name will trust in you, for you, Lord, have never forsaken those who seek you. (Psalm 9:10)*

We will only be able to truly put our trust in the Lord, if we have first drawn near to Him.

> *But as for me, it is good to be near God. I have made the Sovereign Lord my refuge; I will tell of all your deeds. (Psalm 73:28)*

If our religion is mostly theoretical and we lack a **personal relationship** with Jesus, then we will never be able to trust Him no matter how many times we exhort each other that faith in God is our obligation and responsibility. The true Christian life is not that we must **try** to trust Him; it is that through His gracious self-revelation and His indwelling life we **may** trust Him, and we **are enabled** to trust Him.

> **Life Application Point**
>
> Faith in God grows out of a relationship with Him. So, if you need a stronger faith, do not try to "grow faith," but get to know Jesus better – through His Word and prayer.

Remember, there is a world of difference between head faith and heart faith. Head faith is presumption; heart faith is based upon the Word of God that is in the heart of a believer who is walking in daily fellowship with and heart obedience to God. Head faith will fail; heart faith will bear genuine and lasting fruit.

Faith Is Expressed by Words

> *For it is with your heart that you believe and are justified, and it is with your mouth that you confess and are saved. (Romans 10:10)*

There is a direct connection between faith in one's heart and the confession of one's mouth. If someone said he was a Christian and yet continually expressed doubt that he would go to heaven if he died, would that person have genuine faith in his heart?

It is a spiritual fact that the words of our mouths do express what is in our hearts:

...out of the overflow of the heart the mouth speaks. (Matthew 12:34)

It is written: "I believed; therefore I have spoken." With that same spirit of faith we also believe and therefore speak, (2 Corinthians 4:13)

The Greek word that is translated "confess" in Romans 10:10 literally means "to say the same thing as, to agree with." Therefore, when Christians confess their faith in God's Word, they are saying the same thing that God has said. From their hearts they are agreeing with and believing the Word of God.

> **Life Application Question**
>
> What have your recent words been revealing about what is in your heart?

The words of our mouth do not create anything (only God does that), but our words do reveal the faith or unbelief that is in our hearts.

We Are Saved by Faith

One of the most powerful phrases in the New Testament is "the just shall live by faith." This phrase is a quotation of Habakkuk 2:4,

...the righteous will live by his faith

and it is found in three places in the New Testament: Romans 1:17; Galatians 3:11; Hebrews 10:38. **We are saved by faith.** We do not earn salvation, but we receive it by faith. We receive salvation by believing. But, exactly what do we believe to be saved?

Now, brothers, I want to remind you of the gospel I preached to you, which you received and on which you have taken your stand. By this gospel you are saved, if you hold firmly to the word I preached to you. Otherwise, you have believed in vain. For what

I received I passed on to you as of first importance: that Christ died for our sins according to the Scriptures, that he was buried, that he was raised on the third day according to the Scriptures, (1 Corinthians 15:1-4)

Paul says we must believe:

1. Jesus died for our sins.
2. He was buried.
3. He rose again the third day.
4. What Jesus did fulfilled the Scriptures.

These facts necessarily imply a number of other facts:

5. We are lost, helpless sinners in need of a Savior.
6. Jesus was God and able to pay the penalty for our sins.
7. Jesus was sinless and able to rise from the dead.
8. The Scriptures are the Word of God.

However, merely "believing" these truths is not enough by itself:

You believe that there is one God. Good! Even the demons believe that – and shudder. (James 2:19)

We must also respond to Jesus:

…and whoever comes to me I will never drive away. (John 6:37)

but whoever drinks the water I give him will never thirst. Indeed, the water I give him will become in him a spring of water welling up to eternal life. (John 4:14)

Here I am! I stand at the door and knock. If anyone hears my voice and opens the door, I will come in and eat with him, and he with me. (Revelation 3:20)

In addition to believing the truths of the Gospel, we must also **receive** salvation. We must believe **and** receive:

> *Yet to all who **received** him, to those who **believed** in his name, he gave the right to become children of God – children born not of natural descent, nor of human decision or a husband's will, but born of God. (John 1:12-13)*
>
> *That if you confess with your mouth, "Jesus is Lord," and believe in your heart that God raised him from the dead, you will be saved. (Romans 10:9)*

Life Application Point

The Western world is full of "believers," but many of them are not saved because they have never repented and received.

To confess "Jesus is Lord" with your mouth means you surrender to Him as your Lord and God. It means to receive Him as your personal Lord and Savior. It means to turn from your own way and give your life to Jesus. It is at this point that you are "born again" and saved:

> *In reply Jesus declared, "I tell you the truth, no one can see the kingdom of God unless he is born again." (John 3:3)*

We Are Saved by Faith Alone

To be saved it is necessary to respond to Jesus and to receive His gift. Yet, that action of responding is not an act that **merits** salvation; it is merely a receiving of His free gift. We are saved by faith and not by works:

> *he saved us, not because of righteous things we had done, but because of his mercy. He saved us through the washing of rebirth and renewal by the Holy Spirit, (Titus 3:5)*

We do not earn salvation in any sense. Even the faith by which we appropriate God's gift of salvation is itself a gift from God:

> *For it is by grace you have been saved, through faith – and this not from yourselves, it is the gift of God – not by works, so that no one can boast. (Ephesians 2:8-9)*

> *...those who by grace had believed. (Acts 18:27)*

> *For it has been granted to you on behalf of Christ not only to believe on him, but also to suffer for him, (Philippians 1:29)*

Faith is a gift from the Father,

> *...the measure of faith God has given you. (Romans 12:3)*

from the Son of God,

> *Let us fix our eyes on Jesus, the author and perfecter of our faith... (Hebrews 12:2)*

and from the Holy Spirit:

> *But the fruit of the Spirit is...faith, (Galatians 5:22, KJV)*

Life Application Question

Have you ever realized that God gave you the faith to be saved?

Have you thanked Him for that?

There is nothing we do that in any way deserves or earns God's salvation. Salvation is an entirely free gift from God received by faith.

> *Now when a man works, his wages are not credited to him as a gift, but as an obligation. However, to the man who does not work but trusts God who justifies the wicked, his faith is credited as righteousness. (Romans 4:4-5)*

Paul says we either deserve salvation because of our own good works or we receive it as a free undeserved gift; it cannot be both.

> *Where, then, is boasting? It is excluded. On what principle? On that of observing the law? No, but on that of faith. For we maintain that a man is justified by faith apart from observing the law. (Romans 3:27-28)*

Because all men have sinned, it is impossible for anyone to deserve eternal life. So, to approach God on the basis of your works and to try to receive eternal life as if it were something you deserve for your righteous life is to guarantee that you will not receive it. Look at the example of Israel:

> *but Israel, who pursued a law of righteousness, has not attained it. Why not? Because they pursued it not by faith but as if it were by works. They stumbled over the "stumbling stone." (Romans 9:31-32)*

As long as a man tries to earn salvation by his own works, he cannot experience the salvation of God that is received as a free gift by faith alone.

> *For the wages of sin is death, but the gift of God is eternal life in Christ Jesus our Lord. (Romans 6:23)*

Life Application Point

When you share the Gospel with people you know, be sure to speak of both faith and repentance.

"Wages" are what we earn; "wages" are what we deserve. A "gift" is what we have not earned; a "gift" is what we do not deserve. Because all men have sinned, the only thing anyone deserves from God is death, but because of His love, God provided salvation to us as a gift through Jesus' death on the cross. Because it is a gift, we do not deserve it; we have not earned it. We receive salvation as a free, unmerited gift from God; and we receive it by faith. As we surrender our lives to the lordship of Jesus Christ, we believe that God has saved us through Jesus' death on the cross.

Faith and Repentance

Many times in the Scriptures, faith and repentance are spoken of side by side.

By Jesus:

> ...Jesus went into Galilee, proclaiming the good news of God. "The time has come," he said. "The kingdom of God is near. Repent and believe the good news!" (Mark 1:14-15)

By Paul:

> I have declared to both Jews and Greeks that they must turn to God in repentance and have faith in our Lord Jesus. (Acts 20:21)

At the point that a man receives salvation, both repentance and faith are present. The man looks at the sin of his life, in **repentance**, and then turns from his own way, in **faith,** to God's provision of the cross.

In salvation, we turn from the old life with repentance, and we turn to the Lord Jesus with faith.

> ...how you turned to God from idols to serve the living and true God, (1 Thessalonians 1:9)

From this, we see that the true preaching of repentance must always be accompanied by the positive message of faith in God's provision. On the other hand, the true Biblical message of faith must always be accompanied by repentance. Without faith, repentance turns into remorse and condemnation and is fruitless; without repentance, faith has no ground for receiving anything from a holy God.

Faith Without Works Is Dead

While asserting that we are saved by faith alone, without works, we also need to point out the difference between a living faith and a dead faith.

A living faith is spoken of by Paul in Ephesians 2:8-10:

> *For it is by grace you have been saved, through faith – and this not from yourselves, it is the gift of God – not by works, so that no one can boast. For we are God's workmanship, created in Christ Jesus to do good works, which God prepared in advance for us to do.*

On the other hand, a dead faith is spoken of by Jesus in Matthew 7:21-23:

> *Not everyone who says to me, "Lord, Lord" will enter the kingdom of heaven, but only he who does the will of my Father who is in heaven. Many will say to me on that day, "Lord, Lord, did we not prophesy in your name, and in your name drive out demons and perform many miracles?" Then I will tell them plainly, "I never knew you. Away from me, you evildoers!"*

We should never approach God hoping to be saved by our works. We should only approach Him to receive, by faith, His free gift of salvation. However, a faith that genuinely believes in God's provision and submits to His lordship is a faith that will result in outward works. Thus, our faith is not based on works, but works will be the result of our faith.

> *In the same way, faith by itself, if it is not accompanied by action, is dead…I will show you my faith by what I do. (James 2:17-18)*

In James 2:14-26, James gives four examples of how faith should produce works in the life of a believer:

1. Verses 15-17. One believer who says to another "keep warm and well fed," yet does not offer him material assistance, really does not sincerely desire that he be "warm and well fed"! His words were only that: words! There was no substance to them, no reality. It is the same with faith. Faith in God will produce outward actions.

2. Verse 19. The demons believe in the existence of God (in fact, they have more correct theology about God than many Christians!), but that does not help them because they do not turn from their sin and submit to His lordship. In the same way, our faith must be more than mere "belief." It must result in righteous action on our part.

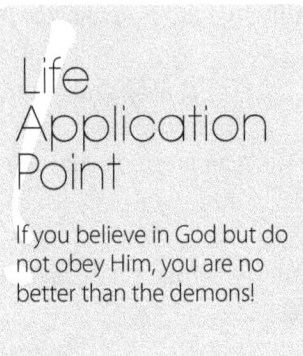

Life Application Point

If you believe in God but do not obey Him, you are no better than the demons!

3. Verses 21-24. Abraham is used as an example of true faith. His faith in God was expressed in outward actions of obedience to God. Thus, it is said that "a person is justified by what he does and not by faith alone." (v. 24)

4. Verse 25. Rahab did more than just believe the words of the spies that Israel was soon to invade and conquer Jericho; she acted on her faith and hid the spies. In this way, her faith produced acts of faith and she too was said to have been "considered righteous for what she did" (v. 25).

It is significant that the Old Testament Hebrew language had no specific word for "faith," but the word that is translated "faith" in Habakkuk 2:4 (the Scripture that is quoted 3 times in the New Testament in the context of justification by faith) is "faithfulness." A man that has true faith will not just believe the right things or say the right things; He will also live in obedience and faithfulness to God.

We are never saved by our works; we are saved through faith, and faith alone. But, a faith that is real is a faith that will produce works.

The Growth of Faith

In Galatians 5, Paul speaks of the fruit of the Spirit, and one of the fruits he mentions is faith:

> *But the fruit of the Spirit is love, joy, peace, longsuffering, gentleness, goodness, faith, Meekness, temperance: against such there is no law. (Galatians 5:22-23, KJV)*

One of the characteristics of a fruit is that it grows over a period of time. That is true of faith.

> *…your faith is growing more and more… (2 Thessalonians 1:3)*

In the Scriptures, faith is spoken of as having varying degrees. For example:

"Little faith":

> *He replied, "You of little faith, why are you so afraid?" Then he got up and rebuked the winds and the waves, and it was completely calm. (Matthew 8:26)*

"Weak faith":

> *Accept him whose faith is weak, without passing judgment on disputable matters. (Romans 14:1)*

"Useless faith":

> *You foolish man, do you want evidence that faith without deeds is useless? (James 2:20)*

"Great faith":

> *When Jesus heard this, he was amazed at him, and turning to the*

> *crowd following him, he said, "I tell you, I have not found such great faith even in Israel." (Luke 7:9)*

"Full of faith":

> *And Stephen, full of faith and power, did great wonders and miracles among the people. (Acts 6:8, KJV)*

"Rich in faith":

> *Listen, my dear brothers: Has not God chosen those who are poor in the eyes of the world to be rich in faith and to inherit the kingdom he promised those who love him? (James 2:5)*

In Romans 12, Paul speaks of the "measure of faith" that God has given every Christian:

> *...in accordance with the measure of faith God has given you. (Romans 12:3)*

So we see that faith can be great or little. How can we then grow in our faith and be strong before God? The answer is found in Romans 10:

> *So then faith [cometh] by hearing, and hearing by the word of God. (Romans 10:17, KJV)*

The following thoughts are repeated from a prior lesson on "The Ministry of the Word of God":

We can see the divine order from this verse: the Word of God comes first, then "hearing," and then faith. In other words, the Word of God is first preached or taught. Then the listener attends to that word with a desire to receive and obey it (i.e., he "hears" it). Finally, faith is produced in his heart.

There are three important things we can learn from this progression. Firstly, it must be the Word of God that is heard. The word of human tradition will not produce faith. Errors and heresy will not produce faith. It must be the Word of God.

Jesus told the religious leaders of His day that the Word of God, which should have been powerful in their lives, had been made ineffective by their human traditions:

> …*Thus you nullify the word of God for the sake of your tradition. (Matthew 15:6)*

Secondly, there must be "hearing." The Word of God falling upon disinterested or disobedient ears will not produce faith. No matter how many books you read, tapes you hear, sermons you listen to, or meetings you attend, if you do not listen to the Word of God with a heart that is willing to receive and obey, faith will never grow in your heart. It will never happen.

This is one reason why so many Christians today are weak in faith. They spend so little time in the Word – and what time they do spend is usually hurried and haphazard – that faith never has the chance to grow. Furthermore, the word that is preached today is often so diluted with man's opinions, theories and misconceptions, that even if you studied it night and day it still would produce little faith.

Thirdly, when the Word is "heard" from an attentive and sincere heart, faith **will** come. As you diligently spend time in the Word of God and listen to anointed scriptural teaching, you will grow stronger in your faith. **It will work.** Your faith will grow.

Paul commended the Thessalonian Christians for their "faith (that was) growing more and more" (2 Thessalonians 1:3). This is because these believers had "received the word" and had diligently obeyed it (1 Thessalonians 1:6-10, KJV).

For your faith to grow continually, you must spend daily time in the Word, as well as time in the congregation of the saints listening to the public preaching and teaching of the Word of God.

But rest assured that your labors will not be in vain. The Word of God is alive and powerful, and as you do "hear" the Word with an attentive and obedient heart, faith will come.

The Christian Life Is a Life of Faith

Faith is so central to the Christian life that Christianity itself is called on a number of occasions "the faith" (e.g., 1 Timothy 4:1).

As Christians we "live by faith" (2 Corinthians 5:7). A "sincere faith" along with love and a good conscience is "the goal" of God's commandment (1 Timothy 1:5). Through the trials and persecutions of life, our faith is "refined" (1 Peter 1:7).

The most famous passage about faith in the Bible is Hebrews 11. Read this chapter for an inspiring list of the heroes of faith from the Old Testament. All these men and women believed the Word of God that was given them and were "strong in faith, giving glory to God" (Romans 4:20, KJV).

Summary

1. Faith is a condition of the heart, not the mind. Faith is not mere mental assent.

2. Faith is present tense, not future.

3. Faith is not sight. Faith believes the Word of God above the evidence of circumstances or feelings.

4. There is a difference between faith and presumption. True faith is based upon the Word of God and is born out of a daily relationship with Jesus.

5. Faith in your heart will be expressed by the words of your mouth.

6. We are saved by faith alone.

7. Faith and repentance always go hand in hand.

8. Faith produces a change in your life. Faith without works is a dead faith.

9. There are degrees of faith. Faith grows through hearing and receiving the Word of God.

Review 8

1. Write out Hebrews 11:6:

   _____

   _____

2. Please give the scriptural definition of "faith" (hint: it is found in Hebrews 11:1):

   _____

   _____

3. Please write "true" or "false" beside each of these statements:

   _____ Faith is not simply agreeing with the Bible.

   _____ Faith is not sight.

   _____ Faith is not feeling.

   _____ To walk by faith means to always react according to what we see and feel in our circumstances around us.

   _____ To walk by faith means to always live according to the Word of God irrespective of what happens around us.

4. Please give a Scripture that relates to each of the following people walking by faith:

   Abraham _____

Mary _____

Peter _____

5. Complete this sentence:

    There is a _____ between faith and presumption. True faith is based upon the _____ ____ _____ and is born out of a daily _____ with Jesus.

6. Please give three Scriptures that show the relationship between the faith of our hearts and the words of our mouths:

    _____

7. Complete this Scripture:

    But as many as _____ Him, to them gave He power to become the sons of God, even to them that _____ on His name:... (John 1:12)

8. We are saved:

    ☐ By going to church.
    ☐ By being good.
    ☐ By faith alone.
    ☐ By faith and works.

9. Salvation is:

    ☐ What we deserve for trying hard.
    ☐ A gift from God.
    ☐ What we deserve for living right.
    ☐ Impossible to receive.

10. Give two Scripture references that speak of both repentance and faith.

   _____

11. Faith without works is:

   ☐ Acceptable to God.
   ☐ A dead faith.
   ☐ Only to be expected.
   ☐ Nothing to be worried about.

12. James 2:19 shows us that if you believe in God but do not obey Him, you are no better than:

   ☐ Any unbeliever.
   ☐ Righteous people.
   ☐ The demons.
   ☐ The angels.

13. The Bible speaks of:

   ☐ Little faith.
   ☐ Weak faith.
   ☐ Dead faith.
   ☐ Great faith.
   ☐ Being full of faith.
   ☐ Being rich in faith.
   ☐ All of the above.
   ☐ None of the above.

14. To grow in faith, you need to:

   ☐ Pray real hard.
   ☐ Never miss church.
   ☐ Hear and receive the Word of God.
   ☐ Hope it grows.
   ☐ There's nothing you can do about it.

The Doctrine of Baptisms

In Hebrews 6, the next foundational doctrine Paul mentions is "instruction about baptisms." Please notice that "baptisms" is plural. There is more than one kind of baptism mentioned in the New Testament; there are no less than four:

1. The baptism of John.
2. Christian water baptism.
3. The baptism of suffering.
4. The baptism in the Holy Spirit.

Before we look at each of these, let us first examine the meaning of the term "baptism" itself.

The Meaning of "Baptism"

The Greek verb that is translated "baptism" in the New Testament is *baptizo* which means to dip or submerge. It can also mean to cleanse by dipping or submerging, or to wash. Metaphorically it can mean to overwhelm (e.g., Isaiah 21:4, LXX). This word is always translated "baptize" in the New Testament except in a couple of places:

> *When they come from the marketplace they do not eat unless they* **wash**... *(Mark 7:4)*

> *But the Pharisee, noticing that Jesus did not first **wash** before the meal, was surprised. (Luke 11:38)*

Furthermore, the word is used several times in the Greek Septuagint version of the Old Testament. Its usage in 2 Kings 5:14 gives us insight into the meaning of the word. The English version reads:

> *So he went down and **dipped** himself in the Jordan seven times, as the man of God had told him, and his flesh was restored and became clean like that of a young boy. (2 Kings 5:14)*

The noun *baptisma* means immersion or submersion. This word is used in the following Scripture:

> *…And they observe many other traditions, such as the **washing (lit. "baptisms")** of cups, pitchers and kettles. (Mark 7:4)*

The most basic root of *baptizo* is the verb *bapto*, which means to dip, immerse or cover wholly with fluid. This verb is used in several New Testament verses:

> *So he called to him, "Father Abraham, have pity on me and send Lazarus to **dip** the tip of his finger in water and cool my tongue, because I am in agony in this fire." (Luke 16:24)*

> *Jesus answered, "It is the one to whom I will give this piece of bread when I have **dipped** it in the dish." … (John 13:26)*

> *He is dressed in a robe **dipped** in blood… (Revelation 19:13)*

In all these passages the key idea behind "baptism" is an immersion or dipping; something is dipped into a fluid and then taken out again.

This is confirmed by Classical and Apocryphal usage of the word:

1. In the fifth or fourth century B.C., *baptizo* was used by Plato of a young man being "overwhelmed" by clever philosophical arguments.

2. In the writings of Hippocrates (fourth century B.C.), *baptizo* was used of people being "submerged" in water and of sponges being "dipped" in water.

3. Between 100 B.C. and A.D. 100, *baptizo* was used by Strabo to describe people who could not swim being "submerged" beneath the surface of the water.

4. In the first century, *baptizo* was used metaphorically by Josephus to describe both a man "plunging" a sword into his own neck and Jerusalem being "overwhelmed" or "plunged" into destruction by internal strife.

5. In the first or second century, *baptizo* was used twice by Plutarch to describe either the body of a person or the figure of an idol being "immersed" in the sea.

6. In the Apocryphal book Judith (12:7), when Judith went out each night and "bathed" at a spring, the word *baptizo* was used.

So, the meaning of baptism is clearly established as an immersion or dipping in fluid. Furthermore, this immersion is usually temporary.

Now, we will examine the four baptisms of the New Testament.

John's Baptism

And so John came, baptizing in the desert region and preaching a baptism of repentance for the forgiveness of sins. (Mark 1:4)

That the baptism of John was different from Christian water baptism is evident by Paul's response to the believers in Ephesus who had experienced only John's baptism:

> Paul said, "John's baptism was a baptism of repentance. He told the people to believe in the one coming after him, that is, in Jesus." On hearing this, they were baptized into the name of the Lord Jesus. (Acts 19:4-5)

This signifies that Paul considered John's baptism as quite distinct from Christian baptism. Furthermore, he obviously did not consider John's baptism sufficient for a believer since he baptized these believers **again** in the name of Jesus.

John's baptism was a baptism of repentance:

> ...John's baptism was a baptism of repentance... (Acts 19:4)

This was a preparatory ministry to make the people ready to receive the coming Messiah. Those who received John's baptism confessed their sins and enjoyed a real experience of repentance and forgiveness of sins, and their lives were changed.[1] However, it was only through the ministry of the Messiah that the people truly received the fullness of abiding, inward peace through the grace of God.

> Therefore, since we have been justified through faith, we have peace with God through our Lord Jesus Christ, (Romans 5:1)

By itself, John's baptism could never give the people ultimate righteousness or peace. Rather, it was to prepare the people to receive and respond to the Messiah when He came. That was the meaning of his baptism.

---

[1] In much the same way, the Old Testament saints had their sins truly forgiven when they offered animal sacrifices in faith and obedience. Their sins were forgiven, ultimately, only by Jesus' blood. Yet, as they obeyed the light they had in repentance and faith, they were saved (cf. Rom. 3:25-26).

Jesus' Baptism by John

> *Then Jesus came from Galilee to the Jordan to be baptized by John. But John tried to deter him, saying, "I need to be baptized by you, and do you come to me?" Jesus replied, "Let it be so now; it is proper for us to do this to fulfill all righteousness." Then John consented. As soon as Jesus was baptized, he went up out of the water. At that moment heaven was opened, and he saw the Spirit of God descending like a dove and lighting on him. And a voice from heaven said, "This is my Son, whom I love; with him I am well pleased." (Matthew 3:13-17)*

John's baptism was a baptism of repentance, but Jesus had never sinned and so did not need to be baptized. John himself recognized this:

> *But John tried to deter him, saying, "I need to be baptized by you, and do you come to me?" (Matthew 3:14)*

However, Jesus answered:

> *…"Let it be so now; it is proper for us to do this to fulfill all righteousness." Then John consented. (Matthew 3:15)*

Jesus was not baptized by John as the outward evidence that He had repented of His sins. Jesus was baptized to "fulfill all righteousness." Jesus was setting an example or pattern of obedience for His disciples to follow. He was showing us by example what He expects us to do. Jesus obeyed His Father in the outward act of baptism even though He was sinless. Even so, we who have been saved by His death on the cross should follow Him in the act of baptism "to fulfill all righteousness." By faith in Jesus, we become righteous, and baptism is an outward sign of identification with Him in His death. So, while John's baptism was a baptism of repentance, Christian baptism following Jesus' example will indeed "fulfill all righteousness." It will complete by an outward act of obedience the inward righteousness which the believer already enjoys by faith in his heart.

Furthermore, Jesus' baptism was also an outward act of consecration to death for the sins of the world. Baptism is a symbol of death and Jesus' baptism was a type of His future death on the cross when He accepted the place of the sinner and bore his punishment. Jesus did not need to be baptized any more than He deserved to die. But, just as His death on the cross was in substitution for the sins of others, so His baptism in water was a consecration to that substitutionary act. In this way too, Jesus' baptism by John "fulfilled all righteousness."

The Baptism of Suffering

> *"You don't know what you are asking," Jesus said. "Can you drink the cup I drink or be baptized with the baptism I am baptized with?" (Mark 10:38)*

Jesus here referred to His own sufferings and death on the cross figuratively as a "baptism." He also indicated that His disciples would be called to experience this same immersion in suffering and death.

> *"We can," they answered. Jesus said to them, "You will drink the cup I drink and be baptized with the baptism I am baptized with,…" (Mark 10:39)*

This union of Christ and His disciples in suffering is also spoken of by Paul:

> *Now if we are children, then we are heirs – heirs of God and co-heirs with Christ, if indeed we share in his sufferings in order that we may also share in his glory. (Romans 8:17)*

> *If we suffer, we shall also reign with him… (2 Timothy 2:12, KJV)*

Suffering is part of the normal Christian life.

Summary

1. Baptism means an immersion or dipping in fluid.

2. There are 4 baptisms mentioned in the New Testament:

    a) The baptism of John.
    b) Christian water baptism.
    c) The baptism of suffering.
    d) The baptism in the Holy Spirit.

3. John's baptism was distinct from Christian baptism and was not sufficient for a believer. It was a baptism of repentance to prepare the people to receive the coming Messiah.

4. Jesus was not baptized by John because He needed to repent. He did it to set an example for us to follow.

5. Jesus' disciples will be called to experience the same "baptism" in suffering and death that He experienced.

Review 9

1. Please name the four baptisms mentioned in the New Testament:

    a) _____

    b) _____

    c) _____

    d) _____

2. The Greek word that is translated "baptism" in the New Testament means:

    ☐ To sprinkle.
    ☐ To immerse.
    ☐ To splash.
    ☐ To spit.

3. John's baptism was a baptism of:

    ☐ Jewish tradition.
    ☐ Repentance.
    ☐ No significance.

4. Complete this sentence:

    Jesus was baptized by John, not because He needed to _____, but to set an _____ for us to follow.

5. As Christians we will be called upon to:

    ☐ Be religious.
    ☐ Lie, cheat and steal.
    ☐ Live a life of ease and comfort.
    ☐ Suffer for our faith.

Christian Water Baptism

To be baptized in water as a Christian was not a suggestion by Jesus; it was His commandment:

> *Therefore go and make disciples of all nations, baptizing them in the name of the Father and of the Son and of the Holy Spirit,* (Matthew 28:19)

> *Whoever believes and is baptized will be saved, but whoever does not believe will be condemned.* (Mark 16:16)

> *So he ordered that they be baptized in the name of Jesus Christ…* (Acts 10:48)

We are saved by faith alone without works of any kind, but a faith that saves will always produce obedience to God. Therefore, we must understand and practise Christian water baptism.

The Conditions for Baptism

The conditions to receive Christian water baptism are as follows:

1. Repentance:

> *Peter replied, "Repent and be baptized, every one of you, in the name of Jesus Christ for the forgiveness of your sins. And you will receive the gift of the Holy Spirit. (Acts 2:38)*

2. Faith:

> *Whoever believes and is baptized will be saved, but whoever does not believe will be condemned. (Mark 16:16)*

> *...what doth hinder me to be baptized? And Philip said, If thou believest with all thine heart, thou mayest... (Acts 8:36-37, KJV)*

When a person has believed the Gospel and turned from his sin, then he is eligible to be baptized in water.

How Soon Should a New Believer Be Baptized?

It is clear from the Book of Acts that a new believer should be baptized **without delay.**

1. Peter's preaching on the Day of Pentecost:

> *Peter replied, "Repent and be baptized, every one of you, in the name of Jesus Christ for the forgiveness of your sins... (Acts 2:38)*

And the people's response:

> *Those who accepted his message were baptized, and about three thousand were added to their number that day. (Acts 2:41)*

2. Philip's ministry in Samaria:

> *But when they believed Philip as he preached the good news of the kingdom of God and the name of Jesus Christ, they were baptized, both men and women. (Acts 8:12)*

3. Philip's ministry to the eunuch from Ethiopia:

> *And as they went on [their] way, they came unto a certain water: and the eunuch said, See, [here is] water; what doth hinder me to be baptized? And Philip said, If thou believest with all thine heart, thou mayest. And he answered and said, I believe that Jesus Christ is the Son of God. And he commanded the chariot to stand still: and they went down both into the water, both Philip and the eunuch; and he baptized him. (Acts 8:36-38, KJV)*

4. Saul's salvation experience:

> *Then Ananias went to the house and entered it. Placing his hands on Saul, he said, "Brother Saul, the Lord – Jesus, who appeared to you on the road as you were coming here – has sent me so that you may see again and be filled with the Holy Spirit." Immediately, something like scales fell from Saul's eyes, and he could see again. He got up and was baptized, (Acts 9:17-18; cf. 22:16)*

5. The household of Cornelius:

> *While Peter was still speaking these words, the Holy Spirit came on all who heard the message. The circumcised believers who had come with Peter were astonished that the gift of the Holy Spirit had been poured out even on the Gentiles. For they heard them speaking in*

tongues and praising God. Then Peter said, "Can anyone keep these people from being baptized with water? They have received the Holy Spirit just as we have." So he ordered that they be baptized in the name of Jesus Christ. Then they asked Peter to stay with them for a few days. (Acts 10:44-48)

6. The household of Lydia:

One of those listening was a woman named Lydia, a dealer in purple cloth from the city of Thyatira, who was a worshiper of God. The Lord opened her heart to respond to Paul's message. When she and the members of her household were baptized, she invited us to her home. "If you consider me a believer in the Lord," she said, "come and stay at my house." And she persuaded us. (Acts 16:14-15)

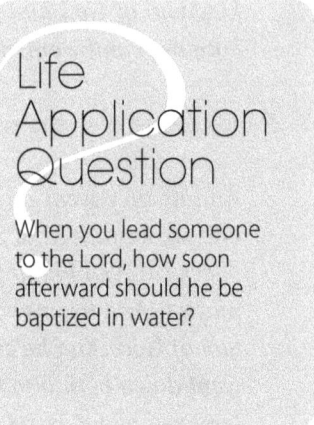

Life Application Question

When you lead someone to the Lord, how soon afterward should he be baptized in water?

7. The household of the jailer at Philippi:

They replied, "Believe in the Lord Jesus, and you will be saved – you and your household." Then they spoke the word of the Lord to him and to all the others in his house. At that hour of the night the jailer took them and washed their wounds; then immediately he and all his family were baptized. (Acts 16:31-33)

8. Crispus and the Corinthians:

Crispus, the synagogue ruler, and his entire household believed in the Lord; and many of the Corinthians who heard him believed and were baptized. (Acts 18:8)

9. The believers at Ephesus:

> *On hearing this, they were baptized into the name of the Lord Jesus. (Acts 19:5)*

We have just looked at every single instance of water baptism recorded in the Book of Acts! What did we find? Without exception, salvation is followed **as soon as possible** by water baptism. The longest period of time between salvation and water baptism in the Book of Acts was three days in the case of Saul (Acts 9:9).

The Nature of Water Baptism

1. New Testament water baptism is **by full immersion.**

    a) See previous word study in Lesson 9 on *baptizo* and *bapto*. The word itself means immersion.
    b) John the Baptist baptized in a certain place near Salim "because there was plenty of water" (John 3:23).
    c) When Jesus was baptized in Matthew 3:16 it was said that He "went up out of the water." The language used speaks of a full immersion.
    d) Concerning Philip and the eunuch, it was said that "both Philip and the eunuch went down into the water and Philip baptized him" (Acts 8:38). The next verse says, "when they came up out of the water..." (Acts 8:39). Again, the language used speaks of a full immersion.
    e) In Romans 6, Paul speaks of baptism as being an outward picture of our union with Jesus in His death, burial, and resurrection:

We were therefore buried with him through baptism into death... (Romans 6:4)

To be "buried...through baptism" obviously implies full immersion. See also Colossians 2:12.

    f) The passing of the Israelites through the Red Sea was a type of Christian water baptism (1 Corinthians 10:1-2); this event clearly signifies full immersion.

    g) Noah's ark was said by Peter to symbolize water baptism in that both are types of our salvation in Christ (1 Peter 3:20-21). This parallel again indicates full immersion.

2. New Testament water baptism is always of adults or children old enough to believe and repent, and it is **never of infants.**

In the Bible, there is neither a command to baptize infants nor any example of infant baptism. Furthermore, infant baptism is expressly contradicted by the teachings of Scripture. The following are proofs of this:

    a) If Jesus and His disciples had been in the habit of baptizing infants, then Jesus' disciples would not have forbidden the little children to come to Him (Matthew 19:13-14).

    b) 1 Corinthians 7:14 refutes infant baptism since Paul would certainly have referred to the baptism of children as a proof of their consecration to the Lord if infant baptism had been practiced.

    c) Conscious faith and repentance are the scriptural prerequisites for water baptism, and babies are incapable of both. Mark speaks of baptizing "believers" (Mark 16:16), and Matthew speaks of baptizing "disciples" (Matthew 28:19); infants are neither "believers" nor "disciples."

    To practice infant baptism is not only unscriptural but is actually very dangerous because it leads logically to the further error of baptismal regeneration. It encourages the parents and the child as he grows up to believe the false notion that the outward act of sprinkling water on the baby's head had some actual saving efficacy associated with it. Therefore, the child will grow up with a false sense of confidence and security that he is right with God simply because of his baptism at infancy.

3. Jesus died only once (Hebrews 10:10-14; 1 Peter 3:18). Since we are baptized into union with His death, we are to be immersed only once (and not three times as some practice).

4. New Testament water baptism is performed **in Jesus' name.** We shall look at every water baptism in the Book of Acts where a name is given:

> *...be baptized, every one of you, in the name of Jesus Christ... (Acts 2:38)*
>
> *...they had simply been baptized into the name of the Lord Jesus.*
>
> *(Acts 8:16)*
>
> *So he ordered that they be baptized in the name of Jesus Christ... (Acts 10:48)*
>
> *...they were baptized into the name of the Lord Jesus. (Acts 19:5)*
>
> *...be baptized,... calling on the name of the Lord. (Acts 22:16, KJV)*

Obviously the clear evidence is that New Testament water baptism should be done in the name of Jesus. Many churches, however, follow Matthew 28:19 for their baptismal "formula":

> *Therefore go and make disciples of all nations, baptizing them in the name of the Father and of the Son and of the Holy Spirit, (Matthew 28:19)*

How do we reconcile this? Jesus told His disciples to baptize "in the name of the Father and of the Son and of the Holy Spirit"; yet, the same disciples who heard that command went out and obeyed it **by** baptizing new believers in the name of the Lord Jesus. There is not a single example anywhere in the New Testament of anyone ever being baptized "in the name of the Father and of the Son and of the Holy Spirit." Furthermore, there is additional compelling evidence that we should use the name of Jesus for water baptism.

The name of Jesus is exalted, glorified and used throughout the New Testament. Where in the New Testament does anyone ever heal the sick, cast out a demon, raise the dead, or receive a prayer request from God in the name of the Father and of the Son and of the Holy Spirit? On the contrary, it is always, without exception, done **in the name of Jesus** (Mark 16:17-18; Luke 10:17; 24:47; John 14:13, 26; 15:16; 16:23, 26; Acts 3:6; 4:12, 30; Ephesians 5:20; James 5:14).

In Colossians 3:17, Paul says, "whatever you do, whether in word or deed, do it all in the name of the Lord Jesus..." Certainly this would include water baptism.

The same apostles who received the commission of Matthew 28:19 obeyed Jesus **by** baptizing in the name of Jesus. They did not make a mistake. The reconciliation is simple.

> *For in him dwelleth all the fulness of the Godhead bodily. (Colossians 2:9, KJV)*

"Jesus" is the name of God, and in Jesus dwells all the fullness of the triune Godhead bodily. So, to baptize in the name of Jesus is to obey the command to baptize in the name of the Godhead. To baptize into Jesus is to baptize into the triune God because the triune God dwells fully in Him. God is one, and all of God is in the Lord Jesus Christ. "Jesus" is the name of God.

Water baptism, like everything else in the New Testament, is always in the name of Jesus. "Jesus" is the name of God. "Father," "Son" and "Holy Spirit" are not names but titles. "Father" is not a name but a title. If you were to ask a child of reasonable age, "What is your father's name?" surely he would not answer "father." Likewise, "Son" is not a name but a title. Proverbs 30:4, says "... What is his name, and the **name** of his son? Tell me if you know!" Jesus commanded us to baptize in the name (singular) of God. "Jesus" is the name by which God has revealed Himself on this earth (Acts 4:12; Hebrews 1:2). "Jesus" is the name of God.

In Paul's teaching about water baptism, he always says we were baptized into Jesus; he never once says our baptism was into the Father, Son and Holy Spirit:

> *Or don't you know that all of us who were baptized into Christ Jesus were baptized into his death? (Romans 6:3)*

> *for all of you who were baptized into Christ have clothed yourselves with Christ. (Galatians 3:27)*

> *having been buried with him in baptism and raised with him through your faith in the power of God, who raised him from the dead. (Colossians 2:12)*

Baptism is a picture of our union with Jesus in His death and resurrection. Jesus is the One who died for us. The Father and the Holy Spirit never died! Jesus is the One who died and then was raised; yet, because the fullness of the Godhead dwells in Christ, when we are baptized in the name of Jesus, we are baptized in the triune God because God is one and Jesus is God. "Jesus" is the name of God.

One of Paul's most characteristic expressions is "en Christo" (in Christ). Paul says the believer is "in Christ." However, because God is one and Jesus is God, we are in the fullness of the triune Godhead when we are in Christ.

All the blessings of redemption are "in Christ"; so, water baptism, an outward witness of the entrance of the believer into union with the Son of God, must also be into "the name of Jesus." In the Bible, the name of God and God Himself are often equated. When you are baptized into the "name of the Lord Jesus," you are baptized into **union with Jesus Christ,** and you are made to be "in Christ" and partakers of the benefits of redemption.

The simplest proof of this truth is that every baptism in the Book of Acts, without exception, is performed "in the name of Jesus."

While recognizing that full immersion in the name of Jesus is the New Testament mode, the spirit of baptism and commitment to the Lord Jesus are of more importance than the exact form. In other words, the most important thing is that the new believer is baptized in water. The mode of baptism should not become an issue of division.

The Meaning of Water Baptism

Water baptism is an outward act depicting what has already happened inside the heart and life of the new believer. Water baptism graphically depicts several spiritual realities.

1. Union with Jesus.

   a) Baptism signifies that we were united with Jesus in His death and burial.

      Or don't you know that all of us who were baptized into Christ Jesus were baptized into his death? We were therefore buried with him through baptism into death in order that, just as Christ was raised from the dead through the glory of the Father, we too may live a new life. (Romans 6:3-4)

> *having been buried with him in baptism and raised with him through your faith in the power of God, who raised him from the dead. (Colossians 2:12)*

When you were born again, your "old man" died. Your old life came to an end. All connection with sin and self was potentially severed. That will become a spiritual reality in your life as you embrace it by faith and walk in it.

We were united with Jesus in His death; we died to sin, self and the power of the world:

> *For we know that our old self was crucified with him so that the body of sin might be done away with, that we should no longer be slaves to sin – because anyone who has died has been freed from sin. (Romans 6:6-7)*

> *May I never boast except in the cross of our Lord Jesus Christ, through which the world has been crucified to me, and I to the world. (Galatians 6:14)*

In our union with Jesus, we also died to the law:

> *For through the law I died to the law so that I might live for God. (Galatians 2:19)*

Sin, self, the world and the law all have as much power over you as they do over a dead body! That is what happened when you were saved, and water baptism graphically depicts it: you died with Christ. The old man is now dead; he has no power or strength unless you give it to him. Victory is yours, but you must choose to walk in it:

> *In the same way, count yourselves dead to sin but alive to God in Christ Jesus. (Romans 6:11)*

> *Those who belong to Christ Jesus have crucified the sinful nature with its passions and desires. Since we live by the Spirit, let us keep in step with the Spirit. (Galatians 5:24-25)*

b) Baptism signifies that we were united with Jesus in His resurrection.

> *We were therefore buried with him through baptism into death in order that, just as Christ was raised from the dead through the glory of the Father, we too may live a new life. (Romans 6:4)*

> *In the same way, count yourselves dead to sin but alive to God in Christ Jesus. (Romans 6:11)*

In union with Jesus' resurrection, we were made alive to God, to righteousness and to newness of life. Again, this is a spiritual reality in Christ. A new life in Christ – a life of victory and fellowship with Him – is ours if we will believe it and walk in it:

> *Therefore, if anyone is in Christ, he is a new creation; the old has gone, the new has come! (2 Corinthians 5:17)*

> *The death he died, he died to sin once for all; but the life he lives, he lives to God. In the same way, count yourselves dead to sin but alive to God in Christ Jesus. Therefore do not let sin reign in your mortal body so that you obey its evil desires. Do not offer the parts of your body to sin, as instruments of wickedness, but rather offer yourselves to God, as those who have been brought from death to life; and offer the parts of your body to him as instruments of righteousness. (Romans 6:10-13)*

> *But thanks be to God that, though you used to be slaves to sin, you wholeheartedly obeyed the form of teaching to which you were entrusted. You have been set free from sin and have become slaves to righteousness. (Romans 6:17-18)*

When this truth of union with Jesus in His death, burial and resurrection becomes a reality in your heart it will produce a radical outward change in your life. Our new life is life "after His image" and His image is an image of holiness, righteousness, truth, humility and godly character:

> *for all of you who were baptized into Christ have clothed yourselves with Christ. (Galatians 3:27)*
>
> *Do not lie to each other, since you have taken off your old self with its practices and have put on the new self, which is being renewed in knowledge in the image of its Creator. (Colossians 3:9-10)*
>
> *You were taught, with regard to your former way of life, to put off your old self, which is being corrupted by its deceitful desires; to be made new in the attitude of your minds; and to put on the new self, created to be like God in true righteousness and holiness. (Ephesians 4:22-24)*

When we were saved, we were united with Jesus in His death, and we died to sin, self and the world. Then, we were raised with Jesus unto newness of life in God. This is the transforming reality of what it means to be a Christian, and it is all depicted by water baptism!

> **Life Application Point**
>
> A daily "putting off" the old man and "putting on" the Lord Jesus is the foundation for victory in your life.

2. Water baptism also signifies the washing away of our sins and the cleansing of our consciences which happened when we were saved:

> *and this water symbolizes baptism that now saves you also – not the removal of dirt from the body but the pledge of a good conscience toward God. It saves you by the resurrection of Jesus Christ, (1 Peter 3:21)*

3. Water baptism is also a public declaration of the new believer's faith in Christ.

   Whoever acknowledges me before men, I will also acknowledge him before my Father in heaven. But whoever disowns me before men, I will disown him before my Father in heaven. (Matt. 10:32-33)

Does Baptism Save?

Over the centuries it has been taught by some that baptism works in a magical way to produce regeneration, and that it secures automatic forgiveness of all past sins and is essential to salvation. The Roman Catholic Church, for example, has taught:

> baptism may be accurately and appositely defined to be the sacrament of regeneration by water in the word. For by nature we are born from Adam children of wrath, but by baptism we are regenerated in Christ children of mercy. (*Council of Trident*, Pt. 2, Ch. 2, Ques. 5)

This means that unless someone has been baptized in water they can never be saved. Therefore, if a child dies before being baptized, he is automatically lost. To deal with this problem, the Roman Catholics have even gone so far as to invent a means of prenatal baptism.

In reply, we say the Bible teaches that water baptism is only an outward sign of what has already occurred within an individual; therefore, only those who have already repented and been born again should be baptized in water.

In Matthew 3:5-8, John commanded the Pharisees and Sadducees to bring forth fruits proving they had repented **before** he would baptize them. Many references in the Book of Acts show that people were always saved **before** they were baptized in water: Acts 2:41; 8:12-13, 35-38; 9:4-6, 17-18; 10:44-48 (certainly God would not have given the Holy Spirit to people who weren't even saved!); 16:14-15, 30-34; 18:8; 19:1-5.

The symbolic nature of water baptism is evident from Jesus' own baptism that could not possibly have been for the purpose of regeneration and cleansing from sin since Jesus was already pure and holy.

Furthermore, the Bible teaches that we are saved by faith alone, without any works of any kind:

> *he saved us, not because of righteous things we had done, but because of his mercy. He saved us through the washing of rebirth and renewal by the Holy Spirit, (Titus 3:5; cf. Romans 2:25-29; 3:28; 4:3-6; Galatians 2:16; 5:6; 6:15)*

Justification is by faith alone and can never be by any outward rite. The thief on the cross was saved by his faith alone (Luke 23:43) and was obviously never baptized.

In Romans 4, Paul teaches that Abraham was justified by his faith alone long before he was circumcised. Abraham's circumcision was simply a "sign" and a "seal" of the righteousness which he already had through his faith (verse 11). Paul wrote this to refute a particular Jewish error of his day which was that connection with Abraham by natural descent and by the bond of circumcision together with the observance of the law was sufficient to obtain the favor of God. Religious man has not changed, and the same error is taught today in a different form by those who trust that participation in an outward act is sufficient to save them (cf. Matthew 23:25-26).

Finally, 1 Peter 3:21 teaches that it is "**not** the removal of dirt from the body" in water baptism that saves us. Rather, baptism is simply evidence of what has already happened in the heart of a person who has believed on Jesus and therefore has a good conscience toward God.

Who May Baptize Another?

Christian water baptism may be performed by any believer. No one is an "authorized baptizer" by virtue of his position or office.

In Damascus there was a disciple named Ananias. The Lord called to him in a vision, "Ananias!" "Yes, Lord," he answered...Then Ananias went to the house and entered it. Placing his hands on Saul, he said, "Brother Saul, the Lord – Jesus, who appeared to you on the road as you were coming here – has sent me so that you may see again and be filled with the Holy Spirit." Immediately, something like scales fell from Saul's eyes, and he could see again. He got up and was baptized, (Acts 9:10-18)

Ananias, "a disciple," baptized Saul. Therefore, since there are no specific instructions anywhere in the New Testament limiting the right of baptism to some special class or rank of Christian, we conclude that it is the privilege of any true disciple to baptize another.

Christian fathers should be encouraged to baptize members of their own families. Those who lead others to Christ should be encouraged to baptize them in water. In addition, women are evidently free to baptize new believers.

The New Testament principle of "body ministry" should extend into all areas of Christian life and ministry such as ministering the communion of the bread and cup, exercising the gifts of the Spirit, praying for the sick, casting out demons, publicly exhorting the church, testifying, sharing revelations, etc.

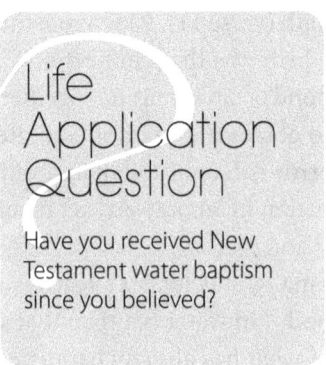

Life Application Question

Have you received New Testament water baptism since you believed?

Summary

1. Water baptism is not a suggestion but a commandment by God.

2. The conditions to receive baptism are repentance and faith.

3. New believers should be baptized as soon as possible after salvation.

4. Water baptism is by full immersion, is done only once, and is always for adults or children old enough to believe and repent. It is never for infants.

5. New Testament water baptism is performed in Jesus' name.

6. Water baptism is an outward act depicting what has already happened inside the heart and life of the new believer. Baptism depicts union with Jesus in His death, burial and resurrection, as well as cleansing from sin. Water baptism is also a public declaration of the new believer's faith in Christ.

7. Water baptism does not save us. It is an outward act performed by those who have already been saved.

8. It is the privilege of any true disciple to baptize another.

Review 10

1. Complete this sentence, and give a Scripture that proves it:

   To be baptized in water as a Christian was not a _____
   by Jesus, but it was His _____.
   Scripture: _____

2. What are the two conditions to receive Christian water baptism?

   A. _____

   B. _____

3. A new believer should be baptized in water:

   ☐ When he feels like it.
   ☐ Never.
   ☐ Without delay.
   ☐ Only on Sunday.

4. Please write "true" or "false" beside each of these statements:

   _____ New Testament water baptism is by full immersion.

   _____ New Testament water baptism is by sprinkling.

   _____ Jesus baptized many infants.

   _____ Only believers were baptized in the New Testament.

   _____ Jesus died three times so we should be immersed three times.

   _____ Every baptism performed in the Book of Acts was done in the name of Jesus.

_____ One or two baptisms performed in the Book of Acts were done in the name of the Father, the Son and the Holy Spirit.

5. Water baptism depicts:

    ☐ Union with Jesus in His death and burial.
    ☐ Union with Jesus in His resurrection.
    ☐ Our cleansing from sin.
    ☐ Our public declaration of faith in Christ.
    ☐ All of the above.
    ☐ None of the above.

6. Does water baptism save us? _____

7. Baptism may be performed by:

    ☐ Only a priest.
    ☐ Only an ordained minister.
    ☐ Only a man.
    ☐ Only a pastor.
    ☐ Any believer.

The Baptism in the Holy Spirit

Speaking of the coming Messiah, John the Baptist said,

> ...after me will come one who is more powerful than I, whose sandals I am not fit to carry. He will baptize you with the Holy Spirit and with fire. (Matthew 3:11)

This was a promise that Jesus would baptize His followers with the Holy Spirit. In this lesson, we will consider this "baptism" in depth.

Who Is the Holy Spirit?

1. The Holy Spirit is a personality; He is not just an impersonal force, power or influence. This is seen by the following:

    a) Personal pronouns are always used when speaking of Him. In other words, the pronouns "He," "Him" or "Himself" are used and not "it." The Holy Spirit is not a thing; He has personality.

    b) The Holy Spirit possesses attributes of personality such as wisdom and knowledge (Acts 15:28; 1 Corinthians 2:10-12). He has a "mind" or purpose (Romans 8:27). He "determines" to do things (1 Corinthians 12:11). He can be "grieved" (Ephesians 4:30). He teaches (John

14:26), and He convicts the world of sin (John 16:8). He appoints, commissions and commands (Acts 13:2; 20:28). Furthermore, the Holy Spirit is said to speak (John 16:13; Acts 1:16; 13:2; Revelation 3:22). All these qualities could not be attributes of a mere impersonal force or power but only of a personality.

2. The Holy Spirit is God. He is equal with God and one with God.

   a) Several triune Scriptures equate the Holy Spirit with God (Matthew 28:19; 2 Corinthians 13:14; 1 Peter 1:2).

   b) Several Scriptures call the Holy Spirit "God":

   *...how is it that Satan has so filled your heart that you have lied to **the Holy Spirit**...You have not lied to men but to **God**. (Acts 5:3-4)*

   *Don't you know that you yourselves are **God's** temple and that **God's Spirit** lives in you? (1 Corinthians 3:16)*

   Now the Lord is the Spirit, and where the Spirit of the Lord is, there is freedom. (2 Corinthians 3:17; cf. 1 Corinthians 12:4-6; Ephesians 2:22)

   c) The Holy Spirit possesses Divine attributes. The Scriptures reveal the Holy Spirit as omnipresent (Psalm 139:7-10), omniscient (1 Corinthians 2:10-11), and omnipotent (Genesis 1:2).

The Need for the Baptism in the Holy Spirit

In Acts 1:8 Jesus told His disciples,

But you will receive power when the Holy Spirit comes on you; and you will be my witnesses in Jerusalem, and in all Judea and Samaria, and to the ends of the earth.

It is clear from this Scripture that while a Christian can be saved without receiving the baptism in the Holy Spirit, he cannot fully realize his calling to be a true witness for Christ without the power and presence of the Holy Spirit in his life (cf. Luke 24:48-49).

> **Life Application Question**
>
> Have you ever tried to live the Christian life without the indwelling Holy Spirit?
>
> How successful were you?

Paul said,

My message and my preaching were not with wise and persuasive words, but with a demonstration of the Spirit's power, so that your faith might not rest on men's wisdom, but on God's power. (1 Corinthians 2:4-5)

He also wrote,

by the power of signs and miracles, through the power of the Spirit. So from Jerusalem all the way around to Illyricum, I have fully proclaimed the gospel of Christ. (Romans 15:19; cf. 1 Corinthians 4:20; 2 Corinthians 6:7; 10:3-4; 12:12; Ephesians 6:10; 1 Thessalonians 1:5; 2 Timothy 3:1-5)

Many today are trying to preach the gospel and proclaim the kingdom of God, but they are producing little real or lasting fruit. The reason for that is simply that they are doing it in their own human strength and wisdom. God's way, however, is "'Not by might nor by power, but by my Spirit,' says the Lord Almighty." (Zechariah 4:6).

In Mark 16:15, Jesus gave His church the Great Commission, "Go into all the world and preach the good news to all creation." However, that is not all that Jesus said. He went on in verses 17-18 to describe the supernatural signs that would accompany the preaching of the gospel:

> *And these signs will accompany those who believe: In my name they will drive out demons; they will speak in new tongues; they will pick up snakes with their hands; and when they drink deadly poison, it will not hurt them at all; they will place their hands on sick people, and they will get well.*

Please notice that Jesus said the signs would accompany "those who believe." He did not say the signs would follow "the apostles only" or "the early church only." Jesus said the signs would follow any believer (cf. John 14:12).

Why is it then that the signs Jesus spoke of in Mark 16 are not following many believers? Is it because it is not God's will for us to experience the supernatural power of God? Was that experience limited only to the early church? To answer those questions consider 1 Corinthians 1:7 where Paul states that God's will is that His church does

> *...not lack any spiritual gift as you eagerly wait for our Lord Jesus Christ to be revealed.*

The Greek word translated "spiritual gift" here is *charisma* and refers to the supernatural gifts of the Holy Spirit. Obviously, God's will is that His church experience the supernatural power of the Holy Spirit right up until Jesus' return.

Is the reason for the lack of power in many Christian churches perhaps because the baptism in the Holy Spirit is not for everyone? The answer to that question is clearly "No" because in Acts 2:38-39, Peter said that the promise of the Holy Spirit

> *...is for you and your children and for all who are far off – for all whom the Lord our God will call. (Acts 2:39)*

Furthermore, in Joel 2:28-29, it was predicted that in the latter days God would pour out His Spirit upon "all people." Clearly then, the promise of the empowering of the Holy Spirit was not limited by God to the early church or to some select group of people, but it is promised to **every** believer in **any** period of time right up until Jesus' return.

Why then is there a lack of power in the lives of many Christians? The answer is simply that while many Christians have truly been born again and have received eternal life, they have not gone on to the second experience of the baptism in the Holy Spirit. One reason for this is that Christians are sometimes taught that they received the fullness of the Holy Spirit when they were born again and that there is no additional experience. This teaching, however, is unscriptural as we will now see.

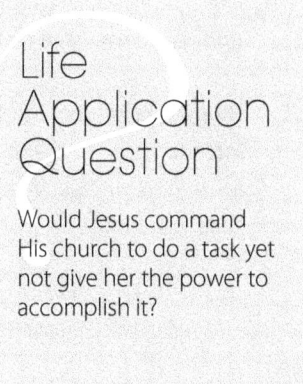

Life Application Question

Would Jesus command His church to do a task yet not give her the power to accomplish it?

The Promise of the Baptism in the Holy Spirit

> *And you also were included in Christ when you heard the word of truth, the gospel of your salvation. Having believed, you were marked in him with a seal, the promised Holy Spirit, (Ephesians 1:13)*

The Holy Spirit was promised:

1. In the Old Testament prophecies:

> *And afterward, I will pour out my Spirit on all people. Your sons and daughters will prophesy, your old men will dream dreams, your young men will see visions. Even on my servants, both men and women, I will pour out my Spirit in those days. (Joel 2:28-29; cf. Acts 2:16ff)*

> *For I will pour water on the thirsty land, and streams on the dry ground; I will pour out my Spirit on your offspring, and my blessing on your descendants. (Isaiah 44:3; cf. Zechariah 12:10; Isaiah 32:15; Ezekiel 39:29; Galatians 3:14)*

2. By the Lord Jesus:

> *I am going to send you what my Father has promised; but stay in the city until you have been clothed with power from on high. (Luke 24:49)*

> *By this he meant the Spirit, whom those who believed in him were later to receive. Up to that time the Spirit had not been given, since Jesus had not yet been glorified. (John 7:39; cf. 14:15-26; 16:7-15; Acts 1:4-8)*

The Subsequent Experience of the Baptism in the Holy Spirit

The Bible teaches that there is an experience of being baptized in the Holy Spirit that is subsequent to and separate from the new birth and salvation.

In Acts 8:5-13, Philip preached the gospel at Samaria and many people received the Word (v. 14), believed the Word (v. 12), and were baptized in water (v. 12). Quite obviously they were born again! However, they did not receive the Holy Spirit until later in verses 14-17, when Peter and John came down from Jerusalem to pray for them. Clearly then, there are two distinct experiences: the new birth and the baptism in the Holy Spirit.

In Acts 19:1-6, Paul came across a group of disciples at Ephesus. These men had already "believed" (verse 2) and were saved. However, Paul asked them,

> *…Have ye received the Holy Spirit since ye believed?… (Acts 19:2, KJV)*

These men had not heard of the baptism in the Holy Spirit; they had only been baptized in water into John's baptism. When Paul discovered this, he baptized them in water again in the name of the Lord Jesus (v. 5; if they weren't saved before, they certainly were now!) and then laid hands on them to receive the Holy Spirit. At no point did Paul even address the subject of salvation because these men were clearly already saved. So, from this incident, we see the example of a number of men who were already saved but who went on to receive the Holy Spirit.

In Hebrews 6:4, we see that there are two distinct experiences of tasting "of the heavenly gift" (salvation) and partaking "of the Holy Spirit" (the baptism in the Holy Spirit).

Paul was born again in Acts 9:3-6 (cf. 26:13-18), but he received the Holy Spirit three days later (Acts 9:17). Jesus never needed to be born again, and yet, He received an empowering of the Holy Spirit in His water baptism in the Jordan River (Mark 1:9-11; Luke 4:18; John 1:32-33; Acts 10:38). Additionally, the 120 disciples who were already born again received the Holy Spirit on the Day of Pentecost (Acts 2:1-4).

In Ephesians 1:13, Paul says the "sealing" of the Holy Spirit of promise occurs after we believe:

Life Application Question

Have you received the baptism in the Holy Spirit since you believed?

> *...in whom also after that ye believed, ye were sealed with that Holy Spirit of promise, (Ephesians 1:13, KJV)*

It does not occur at the same time but is a subsequent experience.

In Galatians 4:6, Paul says it is because we are already sons of God that God gives us the Holy Spirit:

Because you are sons, God sent the Spirit of his Son into our hearts, the Spirit who calls out, "Abba, Father."

In John 14:17, Jesus said, "the world (i.e., the unsaved) cannot receive" (KJV) the baptism in the Holy Spirit. The world, however, can receive salvation! The baptism in the Holy Spirit is not for the world but for believers (John 7:37-39).

Finally, in Luke 11:11-13, we see that it is "children" (i.e., those who have already been born again) who ask their "Father in heaven" for the Holy Spirit.

In view of all these Scriptures, it is apparent that one does not "receive it all" at salvation; There is a subsequent experience of the baptism in the Holy Spirit.

The Purpose of the Baptism in the Holy Spirit

The Holy Spirit brings us into the realm of the supernatural power of God (Acts 1:8; 1 Corinthians 12:7-11); He also comes to be our Teacher (John 14:26; 16:12-13; 1 Corinthians 2:9-10, 12; 1 John 2:27), the Announcer of things to come (John 16:13), the Revealer of God (John 16:14-15), our Leader and Guide (Romans 8:14), the Transformer of our lives and characters (2 Corinthians 3:18) and our Comforter and Helper (John 14:16; Romans 8:26).

The Sign of Having Received the Baptism in the Holy Spirit

The scriptural sign that one has been filled with the Holy Spirit is not a feeling of love, joy or peace, neither is it an emotion, or an anointing, or a feeling of being close to God, but it is speaking in tongues (or in new languages).

Speaking in tongues was predicted in the Old Testament (Isaiah 28:11-12 with 1 Corinthians 14:21-22). Furthermore, it was always the initial sign in the New Testament that one had received the baptism in the Holy Spirit. We will now systematically look at every recorded instance in the New Testament where someone was baptized in the Holy Spirit:

1. On the Day of Pentecost, the 120 disciples were filled with the Holy Spirit and all spoke in tongues.

    All of them were filled with the Holy Spirit and began to speak in other tongues as the Spirit enabled them. (Acts 2:4)

2. At Samaria, when the people were baptized with the Holy Spirit, there is no mention of speaking in tongues. However, it is said,

    When Simon saw that the Spirit was given at the laying on of the apostles' hands, he offered them money and said, "Give me also this ability so that everyone on whom I lay my hands may receive the Holy Spirit." (Acts 8:18-19)

Simon "saw" that the people had received the Holy Spirit. Since the Holy Spirit is invisible, Simon had to have seen some outward, physical manifestation which doubtless was the people speaking in tongues. This was so dramatic that he offered the apostles money to have the same power.

3. Paul received the Holy Spirit in Acts 9:17:

    Then Ananias went to the house and entered it. Placing his hands on Saul, he said, "Brother Saul, the Lord – Jesus, who appeared to you on the road as you were coming here – has sent me so that you may see again and be filled with the Holy Spirit."

Again, there is no mention of speaking in tongues in this verse, but 1 Corinthians 14:18 makes it quite clear that Paul did, in fact, speak in tongues:

I thank God that I speak in tongues more than all of you.

4. When the household of Cornelius received the Holy Spirit in Acts 10, they all spoke with tongues:

   While Peter was still speaking these words, the Holy Spirit came on all who heard the message. The circumcised believers who had come with Peter were astonished that the gift of the Holy Spirit had been poured out even on the Gentiles. For they heard them speaking in tongues and praising God... (Acts 10:44-46)

5. When Paul laid hands on the disciples at Ephesus, they all spoke with tongues and prophesied:

   When Paul placed his hands on them, the Holy Spirit came on them, and they spoke in tongues and prophesied. (Acts 19:6)

6. Jesus' own words in Mark 16 are testimony to the fact that all believers who receive the Holy Spirit will speak in tongues:

   And these signs will accompany those who believe: In my name they will drive out demons; they will speak in new tongues; (Mark 16:17)

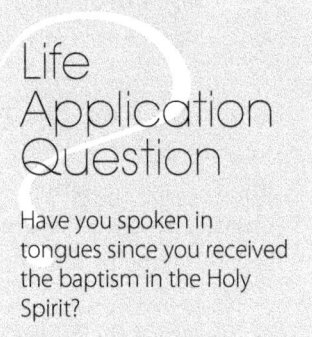

Life Application Question

Have you spoken in tongues since you received the baptism in the Holy Spirit?

From these passages we see that all believers who receive the baptism in the Holy Spirit can speak in new tongues.

How To Receive the Baptism in the Holy Spirit

You may receive the baptism in the Holy Spirit either by the laying on of hands or through your own personal prayer of faith. You do not need to beg or plead with God to receive the Holy Spirit. Neither do you need to "tarry" or wait for the Holy Spirit inasmuch as He has already been poured out upon the church. You need simply to ask God once to baptize you, and He will.

The following are simple and effective steps to take to receive the baptism in the Holy Spirit:

1. Believe that it is God's will to give you the Holy Spirit on the basis of His promises in His Word:

   If you then, though you are evil, know how to give good gifts to your children, how much more will your Father in heaven give the Holy Spirit to those who ask him! (Luke 11:13)

   Peter replied, "Repent and be baptized, every one of you, in the name of Jesus Christ for the forgiveness of your sins. And you will receive the gift of the Holy Spirit. The promise is for you and your children and for all who are far off – for all whom the Lord our God will call." (Acts 2:38-39)

2. Jesus said that God will give the Holy Spirit to "those who ask Him" (Luke 11:13). The reason why so many Christians do not have the baptism is simply because they have never asked in a definite manner expecting to receive the Holy Spirit with the sign of new tongues. Therefore, ask God for the Holy Spirit and believe Jesus' words when He said, "everyone who asks receives" (Luke 11:9-13).

3. Believe and acknowledge that you have received the Holy Spirit when you pray (Mark 11:24; 1 John 5:14-15).

For example, pray: "Father, in the name of Jesus, on the basis of your promise in your Word, I now ask you to fill me with your Holy Spirit. And, I thank you that because I have asked, I have right now received the Holy Spirit. I have been filled with the Holy Spirit, and I can now speak in new tongues. In Jesus' name. Amen."

4. Begin to speak in new tongues. Acts 2:4 says, "**they**...began to speak with other tongues, as the Spirit gave them utterance" (KJV). **You** must begin to speak. Simply begin to speak, except do not speak in English (as you cannot speak in two languages at once).

> **Life Application Point**
>
> You do not necessarily need someone else to help you receive the Holy Spirit. If you are alone, you can pray right now and ask Him to come and fill you.

As you begin to speak, the Holy Spirit will give you utterance in a new language. Do not be concerned about "what to say," but simply begin to speak and the Holy Spirit will give you the words. As you begin to speak, you will find that you are speaking in a new language.

People do not always experience a great "feeling," "anointing," or "emotion" when they receive the baptism. It does not matter whether you do or not. Jesus said that your heavenly Father **will** give you the Holy Spirit when you ask, and He cannot lie. Therefore, simply thank God that He has filled you with the Holy Spirit and begin to speak in new tongues.

5. Continue to pray in tongues **daily.**

   For he that speaketh in an [unknown] tongue speaketh not unto men, but unto God: for no man understandeth [him]; howbeit in the spirit he speaketh mysteries. (1 Corinthians 14:2, KJV)

   He who speaks in a tongue edifies himself... (1 Corinthians 14:4)

And pray in the Spirit on all occasions with all kinds of prayers and requests... (Ephesians 6:18)

But you, dear friends, build yourselves up in your most holy faith and pray in the Holy Spirit. Keep yourselves in God's love as you wait for the mercy of our Lord Jesus Christ to bring you to eternal life. (Jude 20-21; cf. 1 Corinthians 14:5, 14-15, 18, 39;Romans 8:26-27; Isaiah 28:11-12)

Summary

1. Jesus promised that His followers would receive the baptism in the Holy Spirit.

2. The Holy Spirit is not an impersonal force or power. He has personality.

3. The Holy Spirit is God. He is one with God and equal with God.

4. While a Christian can be saved without receiving the baptism in the Holy Spirit, he cannot be a true witness for Christ without the power and presence of the Holy Spirit in his life.

5. The baptism in the Holy Spirit is an experience that is offered to all believers until Jesus' return.

6. The baptism in the Holy Spirit was promised by the Old Testament prophets as well as by Jesus.

7. The baptism in the Holy Spirit is an experience that is subsequent to and distinct from the new birth and salvation.

8. The scriptural sign of having received the baptism in the Holy Spirit is speaking in new tongues or languages.

Review 11

1. The Holy Spirit is:

   ☐ An impersonal force.
   ☐ God's strength.
   ☐ An angelic influence.
   ☐ A personality.

2. The Holy Spirit is:

   ☐ God.
   ☐ Less than God.
   ☐ More than God.
   ☐ Not God.

3. Please write "true" or "false" beside each of these statements, and give a Scripture reference to support your answer:

   _____ The Holy Spirit is called "God" in the New Testament.
   Scripture: _____

   _____ The Holy Spirit possesses Divine attributes.
   Scripture: _____

   _____ A Christian needs the power of the Holy Spirit in his life to be able to be a true witness for Christ.
   Scripture: _____

   _____ God's will is that His church experience the supernatural power of the Holy Spirit right up until Jesus' return.
   Scripture: _____

_____ The promise of the Holy Spirit was limited by God to a small group of people.
Scripture: _____

_____ All believers receive the fullness of the Holy Spirit when they are born again, and there is no additional experience.
Scripture: _____

_____ The Holy Spirit was promised in the Old Testament prophecies.
Scripture: _____

_____ The Holy Spirit was promised by the Lord Jesus.
Scripture: _____

4. Give six Scriptures that show that the baptism in the Holy Spirit is a second experience after salvation.

_____

_____

5. The Holy Spirit comes to:

    ☐ Bring us into the realm of the supernatural power of God.
    ☐ Be our Teacher.
    ☐ Show us things to come.
    ☐ Reveal God to us.
    ☐ Be our Leader and Guide.
    ☐ Transform our lives and characters.
    ☐ Be our Comforter and Helper.
    ☐ All of the above.
    ☐ None of the above.

6. The scriptural sign that one has been filled with the Holy Spirit is:

    ☐ A feeling of love.
    ☐ A feeling of joy.
    ☐ A feeling of peace.
    ☐ A feeling of being close to God.
    ☐ Having a vision.
    ☐ Being caught up into heaven.
    ☐ Running around the room in excitement.
    ☐ Speaking in a new language.

7. If you have not yet been filled with the Holy Spirit and spoken in new tongues:

    ☐ You can right now.
    ☐ You never will be.
    ☐ You might as well give up.
    ☐ God does not like you.

8. Write out Luke 11:13:

    _____

    _____

Laying On of Hands

I have never read a "Systematic Theology" that had a chapter on the "Laying on of Hands," and yet this is one the six doctrines that Paul described as foundational in Hebrews 6! We will examine the practice of the laying on of hands in both testaments.

Laying On of Hands in the Old Testament

The laying on of hands was an established practice in the Old Testament.

1. Jacob:

> And Joseph took both of them, Ephraim on his right toward Israel's left hand and Manasseh on his left toward Israel's right hand, and brought them close to him. But Israel reached out his right hand and put it on Ephraim's head, though he was the younger, and crossing his arms, he put his left hand on Manasseh's head, even though Manasseh was the firstborn…When Joseph saw his father placing his right hand on Ephraim's head he was displeased; so he took hold of his father's hand to move it from Ephraim's head to Manasseh's head. Joseph said to him, "No, my father, this one is the firstborn; put your right hand on his head." But his father refused and said, "I know, my son, I know. He too will become a people, and he too will become great. Nevertheless,

> *his younger brother will be greater than he, and his descendants will become a group of nations." He blessed them that day and said, "In your name will Israel pronounce this blessing: 'May God make you like Ephraim and Manasseh.'" So he put Ephraim ahead of Manasseh. (Genesis 48:13-20)*

From this passage, we see the reality of the laying on of hands. Joseph brought his two sons to Jacob to receive his blessing, and when Jacob put his right hand upon Ephraim, it displeased Joseph because Manasseh was his firstborn. By switching the blessing, Jacob was said to have *"put Ephraim ahead of Manasseh."* Through the laying on of Jacob's right hand, Ephraim received the first and greater blessing. Then through the laying on of Jacob's left hand, Manasseh received the lesser blessing though a blessing nevertheless.

2. Moses:

When Moses was old and about to die, God instructed him to set Joshua in his place as leader over Israel:

> *So the Lord said to Moses, "Take Joshua son of Nun, a man in whom is the spirit, and lay your hand on him. Have him stand before Eleazar the priest and the entire assembly and commission him in their presence. Give him some of your authority so the whole Israelite community will obey him." (Numbers 27:18-20)*

Moses proceeded to do this:

> *Moses did as the Lord commanded him. He took Joshua and had him stand before Eleazar the priest and the whole assembly. Then he laid his hands on him and commissioned him, as the Lord instructed through Moses. (Numbers 27:22-23)*

The powerful result of this action is described later in Deuteronomy:

> *Now Joshua son of Nun was filled with the spirit of wisdom*

> because Moses had laid his hands on him. So the Israelites listened to him and did what the Lord had commanded Moses. (Deuteronomy 34:9)

Through the laying on of Moses' hands, two things were accomplished. Joshua was established before Israel as their divinely-appointed leader, and a measure of the leadership anointing that was upon Moses was transferred to him. Joshua received "the spirit of wisdom" as well as "authority" from Moses through the laying on of his hands.

3. Elisha:

As Elisha lay on his deathbed, Joash, the king of Israel, came to him. Then, Elisha gave the king a prophetic symbol:

> Elisha said, "Get a bow and some arrows," and he did so. "Take the bow in your hands," he said to the king of Israel. When he had taken it, Elisha put his hands on the king's hands. "Open the east window," he said, and he opened it. "Shoot!" Elisha said, and he shot. "The Lord's arrow of victory, the arrow of victory over Aram!" Elisha declared. "You will completely destroy the Arameans at Aphek." (2 Kings 13:15-17)

The shooting of the arrow through the window symbolized the defeat of Syria by Israel. Notice the laying on of hands by Elisha. As Elisha laid his hands on the king's hands, this presumably was a divine appointment, through the prophet, of Joash to be the leader who would bring deliverance to Israel. So, we see again a twofold purpose of the laying on of hands: to acknowledge the divinely appointed leader over God's people and to impart to him special grace and anointing to accomplish his task.

4. Levitical sacrifice:

In Old Testament sacrifice, hands were laid on the victim and the sin of the sinner confessed over it.

> *If the whole Israelite community sins unintentionally and does what is forbidden in any of the Lord's commands, even though the community is unaware of the matter, they are guilty. When they become aware of the sin they committed, the assembly must bring a young bull as a sin offering and present it before the Tent of Meeting. The elders of the community are to lay their hands on the bull's head before the Lord, and the bull shall be slaughtered before the Lord. (Leviticus 4:13-15; Cf. Leviticus 16:21-22 Aaron here, as high priest, is acting on behalf of the whole nation on the Day of Atonement; 2 Chronicles 29:23-24; Exodus 29:10)*

The laying on of hands symbolized substitution and the transfer of punishment. Through the laying on of hands, the liability to punishment was symbolically transferred from the sinner to the victim. In this way, the substitute was said to "bear the sins" of the people, and their sins were said to be "laid upon it" and thus removed.

This does not mean that the actual sinfulness of the people was transferred to the substitute but rather that the liability to punishment was transferred. In other words, the substitute bore the punishment of the people's sins.

So, we see in the Old Testament the laying on of hands was practiced for the following reasons:

1. The impartation of blessing.
2. The setting in place of leaders. The public acknowledgement of them as leaders over the people.
3. The anointing of leaders for service. The impartation of authority and wisdom to lead.
4. In Levitical sacrifice, the laying on of hands symbolized substitution and the transfer of punishment. Again, the idea of impartation is present.

Laying On of Hands in the New Testament

In the New Testament, there are seven distinct purposes for which the laying on of hands is used:

1. To impart a blessing.

   Then little children were brought to Jesus for him to place his hands on them and pray for them...When he had placed his hands on them, he went on from there. (Matthew 19:13-15)

   These parents knew the power for blessing that the Lord Jesus possessed. They also knew that it could be imparted to them and their children through the laying on of His hands.

2. The ministry of healing.

   And these signs will accompany those who believe...they will place their hands on sick people, and they will get well. (Mark 16:17-18)

   Through the laying on of hands by believers, supernatural healing can be ministered to the sick. Please notice that Jesus did not say the sick would be healed instantaneously. He simply promised, "they will get well," leaving the question of timing open. Sometimes healing is received immediately; other times the healing comes as a gradual process. Nonetheless, the promise is sure, and we should stand on it: "they **will** get well."

   Furthermore, the ministry of healing through the laying on of hands was not just given to the apostles or to the early church, but it was given to "those who believe." All believers have this authority in the Lord Jesus Christ!

Jesus had this power:

> *Jesus reached out his hand and touched the man. "I am willing," he said. "Be clean!" Immediately he was cured of his leprosy. (Matthew 8:3)*

> *He could not do any miracles there, except lay his hands on a few sick people and heal them. (Mark 6:5)*

This verse in Mark 6 tells us that the few who were healed in Nazareth were healed through the laying on of hands thereby suggesting that the laying on of hands will work when nothing else will!

> *He touched her hand and the fever left her, and she got up and began to wait on him. (Matthew 8:15)*

> *They came to Bethsaida, and some people brought a blind man and begged Jesus to touch him. He took the blind man by the hand and led him outside the village. When he had spit on the man's eyes and put his hands on him, Jesus asked, "Do you see anything?" He looked up and said, "I see people; they look like trees walking around." Once more Jesus put his hands on the man's eyes. Then his eyes were opened, his sight was restored, and he saw everything clearly. (Mark 8:22-25)*

> *There some people brought to him a man who was deaf and could hardly talk, and they begged him to place his hand on the man. (Mark 7:32)*

> *Then one of the synagogue rulers, named Jairus, came there. Seeing Jesus, he fell at his feet and pleaded earnestly with him, "My little daughter is dying. Please come and put your hands on her so that she will be healed and live." (Mark 5:22-23)*

The early church ministered healing through the laying on of hands:

> *And by the hands of the apostles were many signs and wonders wrought among the people… (Acts 5:12, KJV)*

> *God did extraordinary miracles through Paul, so that even handkerchiefs and aprons that had touched him were taken to the sick, and their illnesses were cured and the evil spirits left them. (Acts 19:11-12)*

> *His father was sick in bed, suffering from fever and dysentery. Paul went in to see him and, after prayer, placed his hands on him and healed him. When this had happened, the rest of the sick on the island came and were cured. (Acts 28:8-9)*

And in Jesus' name we have this power too (Mark 16:17-18).

3. To receive the baptism in the Holy Spirit.

The baptism in the Holy Spirit can be received several ways:

a) Simply by asking the Father to give you the Holy Spirit:

> *If you then, though you are evil, know how to give good gifts to your children, how much more will your Father in heaven give the Holy Spirit to those who ask him! (Luke 11:13)*

b) In a spontaneous, sovereign outpouring from God:

> *Suddenly a sound like the blowing of a violent wind came from heaven and filled the whole house where they were sitting. They saw what seemed to be tongues of fire that separated and came to rest on each of them. All of them were filled with the Holy Spirit and began to speak in other tongues as the Spirit enabled them. (Acts 2:2-4)*

> *While Peter was still speaking these words, the Holy Spirit came on all who heard the message. (Acts 10:44)*

c) Through the laying on of hands.

In three of the instances of believers receiving the Holy Spirit in the Book of Acts, it was done through the laying on of hands, twice through apostles and once through "a disciple" (Acts 9:10).

(1) In Samaria.

> *When Simon saw that the Spirit was given at the laying on of the apostles' hands, he offered them money (Acts 8:18)*

(2) Paul.

> *Then Ananias went to the house and entered it. Placing his hands on Saul, he said, "Brother Saul, the Lord – Jesus, who appeared to you on the road as you were coming here – has sent me so that you may see again and be filled with the Holy Spirit." (Acts 9:17)*

(3) The disciples at Ephesus.

> *When Paul placed his hands on them, the Holy Spirit came on them, and they spoke in tongues and prophesied. (Acts 19:6)*

4. To impart spiritual gifts.

> *Do not neglect your gift, which was given you through a prophetic message when the body of elders laid their hands on you. (1 Timothy 4:14)*

> *For this reason I remind you to fan into flame the gift of God, which is in you through the laying on of my hands. (2 Timothy 1:6)*

We see from these two Scriptures that Timothy received some kind of spiritual gift through the laying on of hands. This was accompanied by a prophecy over him.

From Paul's statement to the Christians at Rome, we can see that this kind of thing was a common occurrence in the early church:

> *I long to see you so that I may impart to you some spiritual gift to make you strong (Romans 1:11)*

5. To commission ministries.

Paul and Barnabas were sent out with the laying on of hands:

> *In the church at Antioch there were prophets and teachers… While they were worshiping the Lord and fasting, the Holy Spirit said, "Set apart for me Barnabas and Saul for the work to which I have called them." So after they had fasted and prayed, they placed their hands on them and sent them off. The two of them, sent on their way by the Holy Spirit, went down to Seleucia and sailed from there to Cyprus. (Acts 13:1-4)*

Through the means of the laying on of hands, along with the prayers and fasting of these men, Paul and Barnabas were commissioned and empowered for the work God had given them to do. Consequently, their ministries had great impact and "God...opened the door of faith to the Gentiles" (Acts 14:27).

6. To appoint elders in the local church.

Paul wrote to Timothy:

> *Do not be hasty in the laying on of hands… (1 Timothy 5:22)*

This was written in the context of some other instructions about elders (verses 17-20), so we presume that Paul here was speaking about the laying on of hands in conjunction with the setting in place of an elder in the church. Before he was appointed as an elder, the man needed to be confirmed as worthy of the position.

Other passages speak of the appointment of elders:

> *Paul and Barnabas appointed elders for them in each church and, with prayer and fasting, committed them to the Lord, in whom they had put their trust. (Acts 14:23)*

There is no mention of the laying on of hands in this instance, but it was likely to have been done.

The laying on of hands in the appointment of elders serves several purposes:

a) Recognition and acknowledgement of the person's gifting, maturity and calling to do the task. They are affirmed in that function before the people.

b) Through the laying on of hands, the person is then separated to do the task and actually becomes an "elder."

c) There is an imparting of additional gifting and anointing to them to accomplish the task.

7. To appoint men for specific acts of service in the church.

> *"Brothers, choose seven men from among you who are known to be full of the Spirit and wisdom. We will turn this responsibility over to them and will give our attention to prayer and the ministry of the word." This proposal pleased the whole group. They chose Stephen, a man full of faith and of the Holy Spirit; also Philip, Procorus, Nicanor, Timon, Parmenas, and Nicolas from Antioch, a convert to Judaism. They presented these men to the apostles, who prayed and laid their hands on them. (Acts 6:3-6)*

It is generally recognized that these men set apart for service in Acts 6 were "deacons." The passage does not say whether or not they were specifically set apart as deacons, so I think the Holy Spirit left it open to use this passage as an example of setting men apart for specific acts of service in the church whether they are "deacons" or not. Through the laying on of the leaders' hands, grace and anointing for the task is imparted. Furthermore, the men are publicly acknowledged to be empowered to do the things they have been asked to do.

> **Life Application Point**
>
> Do not be afraid or embarrassed to lay hands on someone when you pray for them. The laying on of hands is not just a dead traditional rite; it involves real impartation.

"Empty Hands on Empty Heads"

One brother speaks about people laying "empty hands on empty heads." He knew of a woman who went to a meeting where hands were laid on her. She was then prophesied over and supposedly was given "the gift of casting out permanent waves." He told her if she could have gotten the gift of putting them in, she would have had something there!

There are two kinds of "unprofitable" laying on of hands:

1. Mere ritual.

> Some churches have the ritual of laying on of hands to "confirm" people. According to their creeds the Holy Spirit is given at this time. However, this is mere tradition and formality, and nothing necessarily happens. Also, men can be set in leadership positions with hands laid on them. But again, if it is only done as a tradition with no faith present, nothing will be imparted.

In the examples we looked at from both testaments, it is clear that in the Bible the laying on of hands was no mere ritual; it definitely accomplished things.

2. Extremes in Pentecostal and Charismatic circles.

In some Spirit-filled churches, people have hands laid on them for nearly anything with nothing being accomplished. There are many people who have had hands laid on them, often with accompanying glorious prophecies of imparted giftings and ministries, and yet, in reality, the people received nothing.

Let us avoid the abuses and excesses, but let us not draw back from the New Testament practice of the laying on of hands.

Methods of Laying On of Hands

The laying on of hands can be done in two ways:

1. Any believer can lay hands upon a fellow believer as a point of contact to release faith and expect that person to be healed (Mark 16:17-18).

2. There is a special anointing or gift of laying on of hands. For example, there is a special gift of laying on of hands to receive the Holy Spirit.

> **Life Application Question**
>
> What are some opportunities you will have in your life and ministry when you will be able to incorporate the laying on of hands in your prayer for people?

In Acts 8, Simon the sorcerer wanted to have the ability to lay hands on people to impart the Holy Spirit to them:

> ..."Give me also this ability so that everyone on whom I lay my

> *hands may receive the Holy Spirit." (Acts 8:19)*

Then, observe Peter's response:

> *Peter answered: "May your money perish with you, because you thought you could buy the gift of God with money!" (Acts 8:20)*

Peter called it a "gift." Therefore, there is a special gift or ministry of laying on of hands to receive the Holy Spirit.

There can also be special "operations" of the gifts of the Spirit that involve the laying on of hands (1 Corinthians 12:4-6).

So, while all believers can in faith practice the laying on of hands for impartation and blessing, we should also recognize that there are special gifts and ministries that involve it too.

Summary

1. The laying on of hands is one of the foundational doctrines of the Christian faith.

2. It was an established practice in the Old Testament. Its purposes were:

    a) The impartation of blessing.
    b) The setting in place of leaders.
    c) The anointing of leaders for service.
    d) In Levitical sacrifice, the laying on of hands symbolized substitution and the transfer of punishment.

3. In the New Testament, there are seven distinct purposes for which the laying on of hands is used:

    a) To impart a blessing.
    b) The ministry of healing.

- c) To receive the baptism in the Holy Spirit.
- d) To impart spiritual gifts.
- e) To commission ministries.
- f) To appoint elders in the local church.
- g) To appoint men for specific acts of service in the church.

4. We should recognize and avoid the abuses and excesses without drawing back from the New Testament practice of the laying on of hands.

5. While all believers can in faith practice the laying on of hands for impartation and blessing, we should also recognize that there are special gifts and ministries that involve it too.

Review 12

1. The laying on of hands is:

   ☐ A dead traditional rite.
   ☐ Something we should not do.
   ☐ Old-fashioned and outdated.
   ☐ A living, meaningful, effective, Biblical practice.
   ☐ Something we should be afraid of.
   ☐ Something we should be embarrassed about.

2. In the Old Testament, the laying on of hands was used to signify:

   ☐ The impartation of blessing.
   ☐ The public acknowledgement of leaders.
   ☐ The anointing of leaders for service.
   ☐ Substitution and the transfer of punishment in Levitical sacrifice.
   ☐ All of the above.

3. Please give the seven distinct purposes for which the laying on of hands was used in the New Testament:

   A. _____

   B. _____

   C. _____

   D. _____

   E. _____

   F. _____

   G. _____

4. Please name the two kinds of "unprofitable" laying on of hands:

   A. _____

   B. _____

5. Please write "true" or "false" beside each of these statements:

   _____ Any believer can lay hands upon a fellow believer as a point of contact to release faith.

   _____ There is also a special anointing or gift involving the laying on of hands.

Resurrection of the Dead

We shall consider this subject under four main headings:

1. Resurrection was foretold in the Old and New Testaments.
2. Jesus' resurrection.
3. The resurrection of men.
4. The nature of the resurrection.

Resurrection Was Foretold in the Old and New Testaments

1. Jesus' resurrection was a fulfillment of Old Testament prophecies.

> ...that he was buried, that he was raised on the third day **according to the Scriptures**, (1 Corinthians 15:4)

The "Scriptures" that Paul speaks of here are the Old Testament Scriptures. For example, Jesus' resurrection was specifically predicted in Psalm 16:

> I have set the Lord always before me. Because he is at my right hand, I will not be shaken. Therefore my heart is glad and my tongue rejoices; my body also will rest secure, because you will not abandon me to the grave, nor will you let your Holy One see decay. You have made known to me the path of life; you will

fill me with joy in your presence, with eternal pleasures at your right hand. (Psalm 16:8-11)

On the Day of Pentecost, Peter quoted these same verses and applied them to Jesus' death, burial, resurrection and ascension:

David said about him (Jesus): "I saw the Lord always before me. Because he is at my right hand, I will not be shaken."…Seeing what was ahead, he spoke of the resurrection of the Christ, that he was not abandoned to the grave, nor did his body see decay. (Acts 2:25-31)

2. Bodily resurrection in general was predicted in the Old Testament.

JOB:
I know that my Redeemer lives, and that in the end he will stand upon the earth. And after my skin has been destroyed, yet in my flesh I will see God; I myself will see him with my own eyes – I, and not another. How my heart yearns within me! (Job 19:25-27)

In this beautiful Scripture, Job said that even though his body would die and decompose, he knew that in his "flesh" (i.e. his resurrected body) he would "see God." This is a clear prophetic anticipation of the resurrection of the Last Day.

ISAIAH:
Your dead shall live; Together with my dead body they shall arise. Awake and sing, you who dwell in dust; For your dew is like the dew of herbs, And the earth shall cast out the dead. (Isaiah 26:19, NKJV)

Isaiah spoke of his own bodily resurrection along with the resurrection of all the righteous dead from the "dust." His image of "dew" is probably a prophetic reference to the supernatural power of the Holy Spirit that will come like moisture to dry seeds that lie buried in the dust, making them germinate and spring up.

DANIEL:
At that time Michael, the great prince who protects your people, will arise. There will be a time of distress such as has not happened from the beginning of nations until then. But at that time your people – everyone whose name is found written in the book – will be delivered. Multitudes who sleep in the dust of the earth will awake: some to everlasting life, others to shame and everlasting contempt. (Daniel 12:1-2)

The first part of this prophecy refers to the time of "Great Tribulation" on the earth. Daniel says "at that time…Multitudes who sleep in the dust of the earth will awake." This is a clear prophecy of the bodily resurrection of both the righteous and the wicked.

Furthermore, Daniel was personally told by the angel who spoke with him:

As for you, go your way till the end. You will rest, and then at the end of the days you will rise to receive your allotted inheritance. (Daniel 12:13)

The word "rise" refers to Daniel's own bodily resurrection "at the end of the days."

HOSEA:
Come, let us return to the Lord. He has torn us to pieces but he will heal us; he has injured us but he will bind up our wounds. After two days he will revive us; on the third day he will restore us, that we may live in his presence. Let us acknowledge the Lord; let us press on to acknowledge him. As surely as the sun rises, he will appear; he will come to us like the winter rains, like the spring rains that water the earth. (Hosea 6:1-3)

In 1 Corinthians 15:4, Paul said that Jesus "was raised on the third day according to the Scriptures." Here, in Hosea, is a Scripture that specifically predicted Jesus' resurrection "on the third day." Hosea's prophecy was addressed to the spiritual resurrection of national Israel as well as to the bodily resurrection of all believers. All the saved will be resurrected in union with Jesus' resurrection:

> ...God... made us alive with Christ... And God raised us up with Christ, and seated us with him in the heavenly realms in Christ Jesus, (Ephesians 2:4-6)

In that sense, we were resurrected "on the third day" when Jesus was resurrected. Thus, this prophecy predicts our future bodily resurrection as well as Jesus' resurrection on the third day.

Another Old Testament prophecy regarding the "third day" is found in the Book of Jonah. Jonah was inside the fish for three days and nights (Jonah 1:17), and Jesus said Jonah's experience was a type of His body being in the tomb for three days and nights (Matthew 12:38-40; John 2:18-22) before His resurrection.

> **Life Application Question**
>
> Does it surprise you that the resurrection of the dead was so clearly taught in the Old Testament?

3. Bodily resurrection was typified in the Old Testament when Elijah and Elisha raised the dead (1 Kings 17; 2 Kings 4). Furthermore, both Enoch and Elijah were translated from earth to heaven in a wonderful picture of the coming resurrection of the righteous.

4. Jesus predicted His own resurrection in the Gospels.

> *and will turn him over to the Gentiles to be mocked and flogged and crucified. On the third day he will be raised to life! (Matthew 20:19)*

> *Jesus answered them, "Destroy this temple, and I will raise it again in three days."... But the temple he had spoken of was his body. After he was raised from the dead, his disciples*

recalled what he had said. Then they believed the Scripture and the words that Jesus had spoken. (John 2:19-22; cf. Matthew 16:21; 17:22-23; Luke 9:22; 18:31-34)

5. The resurrection of the dead was predicted in the New Testament.

   BY JESUS:
   Do not be amazed at this, for a time is coming when all who are in their graves will hear his voice and come out – those who have done good will rise to live, and those who have done evil will rise to be condemned. (John 5:28-29)

   BY PAUL:
   For since death came through a man, the resurrection of the dead comes also through a man. For as in Adam all die, so in Christ all will be made alive. But each in his own turn: Christ, the firstfruits; then, when he comes, those who belong to him. (1 Corinthians 15:21-23; cf. vv. 35-54)

   BY JOHN:
   (The rest of the dead did not come to life until the thousand years were ended.) This is the first resurrection. (Revelation 20:5; cf. vv. 12-13)

6. Bodily resurrection was typified in the New Testament when Jesus raised the dead (Matthew 9:18-25; Luke 7:11-15; John 11:43-44).

Jesus' Resurrection

The Gospel is the Gospel not only of the death of Jesus but also of His resurrection:

> *Now, brothers, I want to remind you of the gospel I preached to you, which you received and on which you have taken your stand. By this gospel you are saved, if you hold firmly to the word*

> *I preached to you. Otherwise, you have believed in vain. For what I received I passed on to you as of first importance: that Christ died for our sins according to the Scriptures, that he was buried, that he was raised on the third day according to the Scriptures, (1 Corinthians 15:1-4)*

The resurrection of Jesus is mentioned over 100 times in the New Testament. The preaching of the resurrection was the cause of the first persecution of the church (Acts 4:1-3; 5:27-42). The resurrection of Jesus is the foundation of Christianity:

> *That if you confess with your mouth, "Jesus is Lord," and believe in your heart that God raised him from the dead, you will be saved. (Romans 10:9)*

> **Life Application Point**
>
> Be sure you always include Jesus' resurrection in your presentation of the Gospel.

The resurrection of Jesus was the evidence that the atonement was complete and had been accepted by God. We're redeemed by the precious blood of Jesus and not by His resurrection, but His resurrection proved that He paid the penalty for sin fully or else He wouldn't have been raised. It is in this sense that Paul wrote in Romans 4:25 that Jesus was "raised to life for our justification."

> *He was delivered over to death for our sins and was raised to life for our justification. (Romans 4:25; cf. 1 Pet. 1:3)*

We shall now consider some facts concerning Jesus' resurrection.

1. Jesus' body saw no decay.

> *So it is stated elsewhere: "You will not let your Holy One see decay." (Acts 13:35)*

Paul, in Acts 13:35, said that Jesus' holy body did not see decay. Decay, which means physical decomposition and corruption, is part of the curse of sin and is the common lot of fallen humanity (Genesis 3:19; Psalm 49:9). Jesus, however, was sinless; therefore, His body could not experience decay while it was in the tomb.

In Acts 13:35-37, Paul makes a contrast between the body of David (an imperfect man) and the body of Jesus (God's Holy One). David's body saw decay while Jesus' body saw no decay.

If Jesus' body had experienced decay, it would mean that He had been tainted by sin when He died, and therefore, He could not have been an acceptable sacrifice to God for our sins (Leviticus 22:20). If Christ was not raised from the dead without seeing decay, then no atonement was made and we are still in our sins. However, by virtue of His absolute sinlessness, Jesus' body was incorruptible (1 Peter 1:18-19); therefore, Paul continues with the promise of forgiveness of sins and salvation through Him.

> *Be it known unto you therefore, men and brethren, that through this man is preached unto you the forgiveness of sins: And by him all that believe are justified from all things, from which ye could not be justified by the law of Moses. (Acts 13:38-39)*

2. Jesus could not have stayed dead.

   > *But God raised him (Jesus) from the dead, freeing him from the agony of death, because it was impossible for death to keep its hold on him. (Acts 2:24)*

In Acts 2:24, Peter says that it was "impossible" for Jesus to be held by death. In other words, Jesus could not have stayed physically dead. Jesus paid the full price for man's sins when He shed His precious blood on the cross; therefore, once He had died, there was no more penalty needed to be borne by Him in our place.

Jesus was sinless, and death, which is the wages of sin, had no power over Him and no right to Him. Therefore, He could not stay dead, but He had to be resurrected. In justice, the Father could not allow His perfect Son to stay dead.

Jesus voluntarily laid down His life (John 10:18) and bore the penalty for our sins and died, but once the atonement was complete (John 19:30) and God's justice was satisfied, the sinless Lamb had to be raised from the dead. It was "impossible for death to keep its hold on Him"!

A common question in the minds of many Christians is: If Jesus fully paid the price for our sins when He died, then why did He stay dead for several days and nights? Why didn't Jesus die and then immediately return to life? Why several days and nights in the tomb? There are several reasons why Jesus remained dead for several days and nights, and they are as follows:

a) Jesus had to remain dead for a period of time that was long enough to show that He had truly died.
b) The Word of God cannot be broken but must come to pass. Jesus had to fulfill the Old Testament Scriptures, as well as His own words, that He would be dead for several days and nights (1 Corinthians 15:4; Matthew 12:39-40; Luke 24:46; Hosea 6:2 our resurrection is in Christ and in His resurrection; Matthew 16:21; 17:23; John 2:19).
c) Jesus remained dead for several days and nights because God, in His wisdom, simply decided that it would be that way.

3. Without Jesus' resurrection, there is no salvation.

> *And if Christ has not been raised, your faith is futile; you are still in your sins. (1 Corinthians 15:17)*

If Christ was not resurrected bodily, then our faith is vain or fruitless, and we are still under the guilt of our sins and in a state of eternal condemnation.

If Jesus was not raised from the dead, He must have been sinful on the cross, and therefore, death had power over Him and a legal right to Him. This in turn means that He could not have died for anyone other than Himself. Therefore, there was no vicarious death of an innocent substitute on our behalf, and we all must pay the eternal penalty for our sins ourselves.

Jesus, however, was sinless and holy on the cross; therefore, He was resurrected bodily (Luke 24:36-43). Consequently, we are not still in our sins; we have been saved, and we are born again unto a living hope of the complete manifestation of our redemption and of our future union with Jesus in His resurrection. Thus, Jesus' resurrection is the pledge and guarantee of our own resurrection....

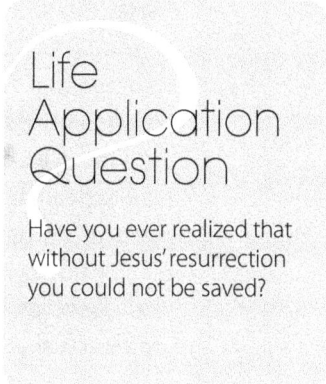

Life Application Question

Have you ever realized that without Jesus' resurrection you could not be saved?

Because I live, you also will live. (John 14:19)

4. Jesus was the "firstborn from the dead."

> *...Jesus Christ, who is...the firstborn from the dead,... (Revelation 1:5)*

Jesus is called "firstborn" in Scripture in several different senses:

a) Jesus was the "firstborn son" of His mother (Luke 2:7, 22-23). Jesus had brothers and sisters (Matthew 13:55-56), but He was the firstborn.

b) The term "firstborn from among the dead" (Colossians 1:18) refers to Jesus' physical resurrection from the dead. He was the first man ever to be raised from the dead with a glorified body, never to die again (Acts 26:23).

The fact that Jesus is "the firstborn from the dead" means more than that He was the first to be resurrected from the dead, never to die again. The expression also refers to the fact that His resurrection has secured the resurrection of His people, and is both the pledge and the pattern of it.

In another spiritual picture or figure, Christ is called "the firstfruits" of the dead in 1 Corinthians 15:20 and 23. The firstfruits in the Old Testament was that part of the harvest that was given to God to represent the dedication of the entire harvest to Him. The giving of the firstfruits to God was both an act of worship and of triumph, for the appearing of the firstfruits at the appointed time gave assurance that the rest of the harvest would be gathered safely in. In like manner, the resurrection of Jesus gives assurance as well as grounds for the resurrection of the full harvest of His redeemed into the kingdom.

c) The term "firstborn" in Scripture refers not merely to birth but also to position, status and inheritance rights.

In Israel, the firstborn son had special rights and privileges including a larger share of the inheritance. In Exodus 4:22 and Jeremiah 31:9, the nation of Israel is called God's "firstborn," meaning that the nation was chosen by God to be the recipient of special privileges and blessings, as compared with the Gentile nations.

This usage of the term "firstborn" as meaning the most illustrious of its class is found in other places. In Job 18:13, "death's firstborn" is a deadly disease. In Isaiah 14:30, the "firstborn of the poor" (KJV) means a pauper of paupers. In Psalm 89:27, "I will also appoint him my firstborn," means to invest Him with royal dignity and clothe Him with preeminent splendor so as to make Him exalted in majesty above all the kings of the earth.

This is the sense in which Christ is called the "firstborn" (Romans 8:29; Colossians 1:15; Hebrews 1:6). The term refers to His position, rank, rights and special privileges.

> *...(Christ is) the firstborn of all creation: For by Him were all things created...all things were created by Him, and for Him: (Colossians 1:15-16, Greek)*

In Colossians 1:15-16, Paul's meaning is that because Jesus is the Creator of all things, He has the position of "firstborn" with respect to all creation. The term does not in any way refer to Jesus being "created" or "born" in any sense, but it speaks of His exalted position and precedence. Jesus holds the rank, as compared with every created thing, of firstborn in dignity and preeminence.

Paul moves from speaking of the preeminence of the Son in the whole universe in verse 15 to His preeminence as Head of the church in verse 18, and he again uses the term "firstborn":

> *And he is the head of the body, the church; he is the beginning and the firstborn from among the dead, so that in everything* **he might have the supremacy.**

So to refer to Jesus as the "firstborn from the dead" refers to the fact that He was the first man ever to be raised from the dead with a glorified body, never to die again. The term also refers to His exalted position and preeminence as the Son of God.

5. Jesus was "justified" by His resurrection.

> *And without controversy great is the mystery of godliness: God was manifest in the flesh, justified in the Spirit, seen of angels, preached unto the Gentiles, believed on in the world, received up into glory. (1 Timothy 3:16, KJV)*

Paul, referring here to Jesus' resurrection, says Jesus was "justified in the spirit." Paul meant that by Jesus' resurrection from the dead it was shown or declared that He always was righteous in His spirit. By His resurrection, Jesus was declared to be the holy Son of God:

> *Concerning his Son Jesus Christ our Lord, which was made of the seed of David according to the flesh; And declared to be the Son of God with power, according to the spirit of holiness, by the resurrection from the dead: (Romans 1:3-4)*

The Greek term for "justify" always means to declare to be righteous. For example, when a Christian is "justified," he is not "made" righteous in a literal sense. Righteousness is imputed to him or charged to his account, and he is declared by God to be righteous. Paul makes it clear in Romans 4 that righteousness is imputed to the Christian:

> *And therefore it was imputed to him (i.e., Abraham) for righteousness. Now it was not written for his sake alone, that it was imputed to him; But for us also, to whom it shall be imputed, if we believe on Him that raised up Jesus our Lord from the dead; (Romans 4:22-24, KJV; cf. v. 11)*

The Christian's change of nature occurs in "regeneration" (John 1:12-13; Titus 3:5). Justification is a purely legal act of declaration in the "Courts of Heaven," whereas regeneration is a transforming act of the Holy Spirit on the inside of the believer.

Many Scriptures reveal the declarative nature of justification:

> *…how can we justify ourselves?... (Genesis 44:16, Hebrew)*

> *…the judges…shall justify (i.e., declare to be innocent or just) the righteous, and condemn the wicked. (Deuteronomy 25:1, KJV)*

> *If I justify myself, mine own mouth shall condemn me: if I say, I*

> *am perfect, it shall also prove me perverse. (Job 9:20, KJV)*
>
> *...he justified himself rather than God. (Job 32:2, KJV)*
>
> *...wisdom is justified of her children. (Matthew 11:19, KJV)*
>
> *But he wanted to justify himself,... (Luke 10:29)*

In all the above Scriptures, the declarative meaning of the term "justification" is quite obvious. In this same sense, Jesus was "justified." By His resurrection from the dead, it was declared or proved that He always was righteous in His spirit (Rom. 1:3-4).

6. Some graves were opened at Jesus' death.

> *And Jesus cried out again with a loud voice, and yielded up His spirit (i.e., His life). Then, behold, the veil of the temple was torn in two from top to bottom; and the earth quaked, and the rocks were split, and the graves were opened; and many bodies of the saints who had fallen asleep were raised; and coming out of the graves after His resurrection, they went into the holy city and appeared to many. (Matthew 27:50-53, NKJV)*

In Matthew 27, the graves of the saints were opened when Jesus died, but their bodies came out of the graves only after Jesus' resurrection. It is likely that God intended this to signify that while it was Jesus' death that conquered our death and opened the door to physical immortality, it is in union with His resurrection that we are raised. Thus, while our redemption was wholly accomplished by the shed blood of Jesus, without His bodily resurrection we could not be saved.

7. Jonah's experience was a type of Jesus' death, burial and resurrection.

> *Then some of the Pharisees and teachers of the law said to him, "Teacher, we want to see a miraculous sign from you." He answered, "A wicked and adulterous generation asks for a*

> *miraculous sign! But none will be given it except the sign of the prophet Jonah. For as Jonah was three days and three nights in the belly of a huge fish, so the Son of Man will be three days and three nights in the heart of the earth." (Matthew 12:38-40)*

The experience of the prophet Jonah was a type of Jesus' death, burial and resurrection. Jesus referred to His physical body being in the tomb for three days and nights as the fulfillment of that type.

In John 2:18-22, Jesus spoke of the same "sign" of His divine commission that He referred to in Matthew 12.

> *Then the Jews demanded of him, "What miraculous sign can you show us to prove your authority to do all this?" Jesus answered them, "Destroy this temple, and I will raise it again in three days." The Jews replied, "It has taken forty-six years to build this temple, and you are going to raise it in three days?" But the temple he had spoken of was his body. After he was raised from the dead, his disciples recalled what he had said. Then they believed the Scripture and the words that Jesus had spoken. (John 2:18-22)*

The resurrection of Jesus' body after three days and nights in the grave was the sign of His divine commission. It was proof that God had sent Him to Israel.

8. We are called to be witnesses of Jesus' resurrection.

   > *God has raised this Jesus to life, and we are all witnesses of the fact. (Acts 2:32)*

Christians have been given a commission by God to be witnesses of the death and resurrection of Jesus Christ (Luke 24:46-48; Acts 1:21-22; 3:15; 4:33; 5:30-32; 13:27-31).

Jesus died on the cross to pay the penalty for our sins, but He did not stay dead. He rose from the dead, and He is alive today. Moreover, He is the same today as He was almost 2000 years ago:

> *Jesus Christ is the same yesterday and today and forever. (Hebrews 13:8)*

When Jesus was on the earth, He "went around doing good and healing all who were under the power of the devil" (Acts 10:38). Jesus is alive, and He is the same today; He is still saving and healing people and setting people free. He is still transforming lives. The only difference is that now He is doing it through His witnesses.

In Acts 1:8, Jesus commanded His disciples to be His witnesses:

> *But you will receive power when the Holy Spirit comes on you; and you will be my witnesses in Jerusalem, and in all Judea and Samaria, and to the ends of the earth.*

Many Christians today are trying to obey that command. However, a great many of them have ignored the fact that before Jesus commanded His disciples to be His witnesses, He told them to wait for the promise of the Father which was the baptism in the Holy Spirit after which they would "receive power." Again, in Luke 24:49, Jesus told His disciples to wait "until you have been clothed with power from on high."

Christians have been commissioned by God to be witnesses of the resurrection of Jesus, and the scriptural way to be a witness of Jesus is through the power of God:

> *With great power the apostles continued to testify to the resurrection of the Lord Jesus,... (Acts 4:33)*

We are to be witnesses of the resurrection of Jesus. We are not called to be witnesses just of the doctrine of His resurrection, but of His resurrection itself! Jesus is alive! Jesus is alive, and He is the same today as He always was. We are to be witnesses of the living Christ!

Therefore, we must have the supernatural power of God in our lives to discharge our commission fully. Without the power of God, we shall be witnesses just to a church or to a creed or to another religion called "Christianity." However, with the power of the Holy Spirit, we shall be witnesses to a Person, to a living Person, the Lord Jesus Christ (Phil. 3:10).

Jesus did not command us to proclaim the "Gospel" to all nations without telling us what the "Gospel" is! A wonderful definition of the Gospel is found in Romans 1:16:

> *I am not ashamed of the gospel, because it is the power of God for the salvation of everyone who believes: first for the Jew, then for the Gentile.*

The Gospel is the power of God for salvation, transformation of life, healing and deliverance to everyone who believes. The Gospel is the redemption of the whole man by the power of God through the death and resurrection of the Lord Jesus. Jesus is alive, and He has sent us to proclaim and to demonstrate His resurrection and His life.

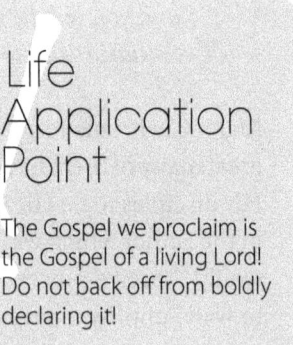

Life Application Point

The Gospel we proclaim is the Gospel of a living Lord! Do not back off from boldly declaring it!

9. The proofs of Jesus' resurrection are many:

    a) The experience of the guards at the tomb (Matthew 28:2-4, 11-15).
    b) The undisturbed grave clothing (John 20:2-10).
    c) The numerous appearances of Jesus after His resurrection. Jesus appeared to:

        Mary (John 20:16).
        The two disciples on the Road to Emmaeus (Luke 24).
        The other women (Matthew 28:9-10).

> Peter (Luke 24:34-35).
> The disciples with Thomas absent (Luke 24).
> The eleven disciples the following Sunday (John 20).
> Over 500 at one time in Galilee (1 Corinthians 15:6).
> James (1 Corinthians 15:7).
> His last appearance at His ascension (Luke 24:51; Acts 1:9-12).
> Paul (Acts 9).
> Stephen (Acts 7:55).
> Many people down through history, including numerous today.

d) The zealous fervor of the disciples who went over all the world preaching Jesus' resurrection. Today our lives should exhibit the same passion for our risen Lord!

e) The change of the day of rest from the Sabbath (Saturday) to "The Lord's Day" (Sunday) in commemoration of Jesus' resurrection (Acts 20:7; 1 Corinthians 16:2; Revelation 1:10; cf. John 20:1).

f) The Christian's own personal experience of faith assures him of Jesus' resurrection.

> *Anyone who believes in the Son of God has this testimony in his heart.... (1 John 5:10)*

The Resurrection of Men

Many men have been resurrected in the past. Both testaments record a number of resurrections (e.g., 2 Kings 13:21; John 11:44). Furthermore, there have been many incidents in history of people who have been raised from the dead, including a large number in this century. However, in all those cases the people went on to die again. Their resurrection consisted in their physical body being restored to life. This is not the nature of the final resurrection. In the final resurrection, men and women will be resurrected bodily never to die again. Many Scriptures reveal that both the righteous and the lost will be resurrected bodily:

> *Multitudes who sleep in the dust of the earth will awake: some to everlasting life, others to shame and everlasting contempt. (Daniel 12:2)*

> *Do not be amazed at this, for a time is coming when all who are in their graves will hear his voice and come out – those who have done good will rise to live, and those who have done evil will rise to be condemned. (John 5:28-29)*

> *and I have the same hope in God as these men, that there will be a resurrection of both the righteous and the wicked. (Acts 24:15)*

> *(The rest of the dead did not come to life until the thousand years were ended.) This is the first resurrection. Blessed and holy are those who have part in the first resurrection. The second death has no power over them, but they will be priests of God and of Christ and will reign with him for a thousand years. (Revelation 20:5-6)*

In addition to the above Scriptures, the bodily resurrection of the righteous is confirmed elsewhere in Scripture. For example:

> *And this is the will of him who sent me, that I shall lose none of all that he has given me, but raise them up at the last day. For my Father's will is that everyone who looks to the Son and believes in him shall have eternal life, and I will raise him up at the last day. (John 6:39-40)*

> *Jesus said to her, "I am the resurrection and the life. He who believes in me will live, even though he dies; and whoever lives and believes in me will never die. Do you believe this?" (John 11:25-26)*

> *Not only so, but we ourselves, who have the firstfruits of the Spirit, groan inwardly as we wait eagerly for our adoption as sons, the redemption of our bodies. (Romans 8:23)*

The bodily resurrection of the lost is taught also by the following passages:

> *If your right eye causes you to sin, gouge it out and throw it away. It is better for you to lose one part of your body than for your whole body to be thrown into hell. And if your right hand causes you to sin, cut it off and throw it away. It is better for you to lose one part of your body than for your whole body to go into hell. (Matthew 5:29-30)*

> *… be afraid of the One who can destroy both soul and body in hell. (Matthew 10:28)*

Jesus taught that the "body" of a man will be cast into eternal hell.

> *The sea gave up the dead that were in it, and death and Hades gave up the dead that were in them, and each person was judged according to what he had done. (Revelation 20:13)*

The fact that the sea will give up the dead which are in it means their bodies will be resurrected.

The Nature of the Resurrection

The resurrection of the dead is not merely a "spiritual" resurrection in the sense of the spirit of a man living forever, but it will be a "bodily" resurrection.

Jesus' own resurrection was a bodily resurrection,

> *Look at my hands and my feet. It is I myself! Touch me and see; a ghost does not have flesh and bones, as you see I have. (Luke 24:39)*

and our future resurrection is said to be in the likeness of Jesus' resurrection:

> *If we have been united with him like this in his death, we will certainly also be united with him in his resurrection. (Romans 6:5)*

> *(Jesus), by the power that enables him to bring everything under his control, will transform our lowly bodies so that they will be like his glorious body. (Philippians 3:21)*

> *Dear friends, now we are children of God, and what we will be has not yet been made known. But we know that when he appears, we shall be like him, for we shall see him as he is. (1 John 3:2; cf. Romans 8:11; 2 Corinthians 4:14; Ephesians 1:19-20; Philippians 3:10-11)*

When the righteous are resurrected, their bodies will be instantly and supernaturally changed into a new kind of body. This will happen at the time of Jesus' return to the earth. The righteous who are alive on the earth at that time will be "raptured" and their bodies will be changed:

> *For the Lord himself will come down from heaven, with a loud command, with the voice of the archangel and with the trumpet call of God, and the dead in Christ will rise first. After that, we who are still alive and are left will be caught up together with them in the clouds to meet the Lord in the air. And so we will be with the Lord forever. (1 Thessalonians 4:16-17)*

> *Listen, I tell you a mystery: We will not all sleep, but we will all be changed – in a flash, in the twinkling of an eye, at the last trumpet. For the trumpet will sound, the dead will be raised imperishable, and we will be changed. (1 Corinthians 15:51-52)*

The lost will be resurrected after the Millennium at the time of the Great White Throne Judgment:

> *...They (the righteous) came to life and reigned with Christ a thousand years. (The rest of the dead did not come to life until the thousand years were ended.) This is the first resurrection. (Revelation 20:4-5)*

> *Then I saw a great white throne and him who was seated on it. Earth and sky fled from his presence, and there was no place for*

them. And I saw the dead, great and small, standing before the throne, and books were opened. Another book was opened, which is the book of life. The dead were judged according to what they had done as recorded in the books. The sea gave up the dead that were in it, and death and Hades gave up the dead that were in them, and each person was judged according to what he had done. (Revelation 20:11-13)

The Glorified Bodies of the Resurrection

The fact that the righteous will be given new, glorified bodies is confirmed by Jesus in Matthew 22:

Jesus replied, "You are in error because you do not know the Scriptures or the power of God. At the resurrection people will neither marry nor be given in marriage; they will be like the angels in heaven. But about the resurrection of the dead – have you not read what God said to you, 'I am the God of Abraham, the God of Isaac, and the God of Jacob'? He is not the God of the dead but of the living." (Matthew 22:29-32)

The nature of our new bodies is described at length by Paul in 1 Corinthians 15:

But someone may ask, "How are the dead raised? With what kind of body will they come?" How foolish! What you sow does not come to life unless it dies. When you sow, you do not plant the body that will be, but just a seed, perhaps of wheat or of something else. But God gives it a body as he has determined, and to each kind of seed he gives its own body. (1 Corinthians 15:35-38)

From these verses, we see that while there is a direct continuity between the body that is buried and the body that is resurrected, the resurrected body will undergo definite and obvious changes.

> *All flesh is not the same: Men have one kind of flesh, animals have another, birds another and fish another. There are also heavenly bodies and there are earthly bodies; but the splendor of the heavenly bodies is one kind, and the splendor of the earthly bodies is another. (1 Corinthians 15:39-40)*

Paul points out here that there is already a precedent in nature for the idea of different kinds of bodies. Our glorified bodies will be different from our natural, fleshly bodies.

> *The sun has one kind of splendor, the moon another and the stars another; and star differs from star in splendor. So will it be with the resurrection of the dead... (1 Corinthians 15:41-42)*

Paul states that there will be a difference between the glorified bodies of the redeemed. They will all be the same kind of glorified body, but there will be many different orders of glory among them. This same idea is found in Daniel 12:

> *Those who are wise will shine like the brightness of the heavens, and those who lead many to righteousness, like the stars for ever and ever. (Daniel 12:3)*

Then, in 1 Corinthians 15, Paul goes on concerning the resurrection of our bodies:

> *So will it be with the resurrection of the dead. The body that is sown is perishable, it is raised imperishable; it is sown in dishonor, it is raised in glory; it is sown in weakness, it is raised in power; it is sown a natural body, it is raised a spiritual body. If there is a natural body, there is also a spiritual body.... For the perishable must clothe itself with the imperishable, and the mortal with immortality. (1 Corinthians 15:42-53)*

Paul speaks of five distinctive changes that will happen to the bodies of the righteous when they are resurrected:

1. The present body is perishable. It is subject to sickness, decay and old age. The new body will be imperishable and free from all these things.

2. The old body is a body of "dishonor." Its physical needs and limitations are, in a sense, a humiliation to man and a reminder of his fallen, sinful state. Paul calls our bodies "lowly" in Philippians:

    (God) will transform our lowly bodies... (Philippians 3:21)

    In contrast, the new body will have beauty and glory and be free from all of man's present limitations.

> **Life Application Point**
>
> Let the hope of such a glorious future resurrection fill your heart with both expectation for Jesus' return and consecration now for the task at hand.

3. The present body dies in "weakness," but the new body will come forth from the grave by the supernatural power of God.

4. The old body is a "natural" body and is "of the dust of the earth" (v. 47), but the new body is a "spiritual body." This is not a "spirit body" but a body made of "spiritual material." In His glorified body, Jesus could walk through closed doors. He could travel at will. He could disappear if He wanted to. He could ascend to heaven and descend again to earth. He could eat if He wanted to for the enjoyment, but did not have to for the sake of His body. In all these respects and in others not yet revealed, we will have the same kind of body that Jesus has!

5. The present body is "mortal" and subject to death. The new body will be "immortal" and incapable of death.

But what about the bodies of the lost? With what kind of body will they be resurrected? We do not have the same extent of revelation concerning that, but we do have a little:

Multitudes who sleep in the dust of the earth will awake: some to everlasting life, others to shame and everlasting contempt. (Daniel 12:2)

If your right eye causes you to sin, gouge it out and throw it away. It is better for you to lose one part of your body than for your whole body to be thrown into hell. And if your right hand causes you to sin, cut it off and throw it away. It is better for you to lose one part of your body than for your whole body to go into hell. (Matthew 5:29-30)

Several things are clear from these verses. Firstly, the resurrected body of the lost will be one of "shame and contempt." Secondly, it will be a body capable of suffering the most agonizing pain and torment possible. Thirdly, it will be an enduring body. The sufferings of hell will not consume it and bring it to an end, but the bodily sufferings of the lost will endure for eternity.

Summary

1. Jesus' resurrection and the resurrection of the dead in a general sense were foretold in both testaments.

2. The resurrection of Jesus is the foundation of Christianity and is a central part of the Gospel.

3. Concerning Jesus' resurrection:

    a) His body saw no corruption.
    b) He could not have stayed dead.
    c) His resurrection was necessary for our salvation.
    d) He was the "firstborn" from the dead, and the "firstfruits" of the great harvest of the redeemed.
    e) His resurrection "justified" Him or proved that He was righteous all along.

- f) A number of people were raised from the dead at the time of Jesus' resurrection.
- g) Jonah's experience was a type of Jesus' death, burial and resurrection.
- h) We are called to be witnesses of Jesus' resurrection in the power of the Spirit of God.
- i) There were many proofs of Jesus' resurrection.

4. Both the righteous and the lost will be resurrected bodily.

5. The resurrection of the righteous will occur at the time of Jesus' return, at which time the righteous who are living on the earth will be raptured. The resurrection of the lost will occur after the Millennium at the time of the Great White Throne Judgment.

6. The bodies of the righteous will be changed into spiritual glorified bodies. These bodies will be imperishable, glorious, powerful, spiritual and immortal.

7. The bodies of the lost will be shameful, capable of suffering pain, and eternal in endurance.

Review 13

1. Give a passage from the Old Testament that specifically predicted Jesus' resurrection:

   _____

2. Give three passages from the Old Testament that predicted bodily resurrection in general:

   _____   _____   _____

3. True or false? Jesus predicted His own resurrection. _____

4. Give three passages from the New Testament that predicted the bodily resurrection of the dead:

   _____   _____   _____

5. Please write "true" or "false" beside each of these statements:

   _____ The Gospel is the Gospel not only of the death of Jesus but also of His resurrection.

   _____ The resurrection of Jesus is the foundation of Christianity.

   _____ It does not matter whether or not we include Jesus' resurrection in our presentation of the Gospel.

   _____ The resurrection of Jesus was the evidence that the atonement was complete and had been accepted by God.

6. Why did Jesus' body see no corruption in the tomb?

    ☐ Because He was sinless.
    ☐ Because He was not there long enough.
    ☐ Because of the cool air in the tomb.
    ☐ Because of the special spices they used to anoint Him.

7. Please write "true" or "false" beside each of these statements:

    _____ Jesus could not have stayed dead because He was sinless.

    _____ Without Jesus' resurrection there is no salvation.

    _____ When Paul says Jesus was "justified in the spirit," he meant that by Jesus' resurrection it was shown that He always was righteous in His spirit.

    _____ To be effective witnesses of Jesus' resurrection, we need the power of God in our lives.

8. Please give four proofs of Jesus' resurrection:

    A. _____

    B. _____

    C. _____

    D. _____

9. Give four Scriptures that teach the bodily resurrection of the lost:

    _____

    _____

10. Regarding the resurrection of the righteous, beside each of these words write whether it is a characteristic of the old body or the new one:

   Perishable   _____
   Imperishable   _____
   Dishonor   _____
   Weakness   _____
   Power   _____
   Natural   _____
   Spiritual   _____
   Mortal   _____
   Immortal   _____

Eternal Judgment

> *Just as man is destined to die once, and after that to face judgment, (Hebrews 9:27)*

There are two things that are certain to happen to every man: death and judgment. No one can escape from either of these.[2]

> *In the past God overlooked such ignorance, but now he commands all people everywhere to repent. For he has set a day when he will judge the world with justice by the man he has appointed. He has given proof of this to all men by raising him from the dead. (Acts 17:30-31)*

God will one day "judge the world with justice." That is why He commands all men to repent – because all men will be judged.

It is not just fallen man who will be judged, but all Christians will be judged too:

> *You, then, why do you judge your brother? Or why do you look down on your brother? For we will all stand before God's judgment seat. (Romans 14:10)*

As we saw in our last lesson, all men, saved and lost, will be resurrected, and after their resurrection, they will face judgment.

---

[2] With the exception of those who will be raptured at Christ's return and, thus, never "die."

> *For we must all appear before the judgment seat of Christ, that each one may receive what is due him for the things done while in the body, whether good or bad. (2 Corinthians 5:10)*

Paul says that man's judgment will be of "the things done while in the body." This is why the resurrection of the body comes first. Man will be resurrected bodily and restored to his original state of wholeness – spirit, soul, mind and body – and then he will give an account for the actions he did while physically alive on the earth.

The Nature of Sin

Sin can be against other men:

> *If your brother sins against you... (Matthew 18:15; cf. v. 21; Genesis 42:22)*

Sin can be against yourself:

> *...these sinners against their own souls... (Numbers 16:38, KJV; cf. Proverbs 6:32; 8:36; Jeremiah 44:7)*

However, all sin is ultimately against God:

> *If anyone sins and is unfaithful to the Lord by deceiving his neighbor... (Leviticus 6:2)*

> *Against you, you only, have I sinned and done what is evil in your sight... (Psalm 51:4; Cf. Genesis 20:6; 39:9; Leviticus 5:19; Numbers 5:6-7; 2 Sam. 12:9-10, 13; Ezra 10:2; Psalm 5:10; Jeremiah 14:20; 44:23; 51:5; Micah 7:9; Ephesians 1:17; Luke 15:21 "against heaven," i.e., against God)*

Sin is not just a passive weakness or simple imperfection in man. Sin is, in a sense, actively and violently opposed to God Himself. All sin is "against God," and this is why sin must be confessed to God. He is the One who will judge man for his sin, and He is the One who forgives sin:

> ...Who can forgive sins but God alone? (Mark 2:7)

Sin is a violent contradiction to and "opposer" of God – of His own Being. All sin is a violation of God's own nature and being, and therefore, all sin must be punished by God.

> **Life Application Question**
>
> Sin is awful to a holy God. Is there anything displeasing to Him in your life now?

"Punishment is the constitutional reaction of God's being against moral evil – the self-assertion of infinite holiness against its antagonist and would-be destroyer. In God this demand is devoid of all passion, and is consistent with infinite benevolence. It is a demand that cannot be evaded, since the holiness from which it springs is unchanging." (From Strong's *Systematic Theology*.)

> For the wrath of God is revealed from heaven against all ungodliness and unrighteousness of men, who hold the truth in unrighteousness; (Rom. 1:18)

God's wrath and righteous anger will be poured out upon all sin and upon all sinners. All men, rich and poor, great and small, famous and unknown, have sinned against God and are under His wrath. No one can escape. This is why God commands all men everywhere to repent (Acts 17:30) and why all men must be born again (John 3:3, 7).

God will not compromise with sin; He cannot compromise with sin. Light does not ever compromise with darkness. It extinguishes it. God does not ever compromise with sin. He punishes it.

Sin will be punished. All men have sinned. Therefore, all men are, from conception, abiding under the punishment of sin – the eternal punishment of sin. But for God's gracious provision of forgiveness through the cross, this is the condition of all mankind: lost forever, without hope.

God Is the Judge of All

The Scriptures present God as the moral Judge of the universe:

> ...*Will not the Judge of all the earth do right? (Genesis 18:25)*
>
> *And the heavens proclaim his righteousness, for God himself is judge. (Psalm 50:6)*
>
> *You have come to God, the judge of all men... (Hebrews 12:23; Cf. Psalm 9:8; 58:11; 94:2; Romans 2:5-6)*

> **Life Application Point**
>
> Let this truth bring the fear of God to your heart. One day you **will** give account for your life!

Unrighteous judges may ignore sin, but God is a righteous Judge. God will not ever forget about sin and act as if it never happened. God will always punish sin, even the least sin. By the necessity of His own nature and being, God must punish sin.

God is perfectly just and righteous. As such, He must give to everyone his due with unvarying impartiality:

> *For the Son of Man is going to come in his Father's glory with his angels, and then he will reward each person according to what he has done. (Matthew 16:27; Cf. Nehemiah 9:33; Job 8:3, 20; 34:10-12; Proverbs 24:12; Jeremiah 17:10; 32:19; Romans 2:6)*

This does not mean that God enjoys punishing sinful man. Rather, the Scripture presents God as longsuffering, merciful and slow to judge.

Ezekiel 18:32 reveals the heart of God:

> *For I take no pleasure in the death of anyone, declares the Sovereign Lord. Repent and live!*

> *The Lord is not slow in keeping his promise, as some understand slowness. He is patient with you, not wanting anyone to perish, but everyone to come to repentance. (2 Peter 3:9; cf. Psalm 86:5, 15; 100:5; Jeremiah 4:27-28; Lamentations 3:31-33; Ezekiel 18:23; 31:15; Matthew 18:14; Luke 6:35; 19:41-44; John 3:17; 1 Timothy 2:3-4; 2 Peter 3:9b; 1 John 4:8b)*

God does not enjoy judging sinful men, but He will do it nevertheless.

The Principles of Divine Judgment

1. God will judge all men.

   > *...a Father who judges each man's work impartially... (1 Peter 1:17)*

   > *...his righteous judgment will be revealed. God "will give to each person according to what he has done." (Romans 2:5-6)*

   No one will escape. Flattery or bribery will not work. Every man, woman and child who has ever lived will be judged.

2. God's judgment is according to truth.

   > *Now we know that God's judgment against those who do such things is based on truth. (Romans 2:2)*

   Man's judgment can be based upon a multitude of things, but God's judgment is consistent; it is always according to truth.

Jesus said that God's Word is truth (John 17:17), so God's judgment is according to His Word:

> *As for the person who hears my words but does not keep them, I do not judge him. For I did not come to judge the world, but to save it. There is a judge for the one who rejects me and does not accept my words; that very word which I spoke will condemn him at the last day. (John 12:47-48)*

All men will one day be judged by the impartial, unchanging standard of the Word of God.

3. God will judge every man's deeds.

> *God "will give to each person according to what he has done." (Romans 2:6)*

> *...a Father who judges each man's work impartially... (1 Peter 1:17)*

> *But I tell you that men will have to give account on the day of judgment for every careless word they have spoken. For by your words you will be acquitted, and by your words you will be condemned. (Matthew 12:36-37)*

Life Application Question

Modern individualistic man often thinks that he is "different" – that he will somehow escape what happens to everyone else. Will he?

Revelation 20:12 gives an account of the final judgment:

> *And I saw the dead, great and small, standing before the throne, and books were opened...The dead were judged according to what they had done as recorded in the books.*

The "books" described here are apparently the records of the deeds of all the lost. No act will be forgotten or hidden. Everything will be disclosed and judged.

> *Behold, I am coming soon! My reward is with me, and I will give to everyone according to what he has done. (Revelation 22:12)*

4. God will judge the hidden motives of the heart.

   > *For God will bring every deed into judgment, including every hidden thing, whether it is good or evil. (Ecclesiastes 12:14)*

   > *This will take place on the day when God will judge men's secrets through Jesus Christ, as my gospel declares. (Romans 2:16)*

   > *Therefore judge nothing before the appointed time; wait till the Lord comes. He will bring to light what is hidden in darkness and will expose the motives of men's hearts.... (1 Corinthians 4:5)*

God will not only judge the outward actions of men; He will also judge every thought, intention and motive of their hearts.

> *Nothing in all creation is hidden from God's sight. Everything is uncovered and laid bare before the eyes of him to whom we must give account. (Hebrews 4:13)*

Life Application Point

Live an inwardly pure life now. We can often fool one another, but no one will fool God on the Last Day!

5. God will judge without partiality.

   > *...a Father who judges each man's work impartially... (1 Peter 1:17)*

When men judge one another, they are often influenced by outward things such as race, physical appearance, education, wealth, social position, profession, etc. However, when God judges men, He will not be influenced by any of these things. His judgment will be perfect and impartial.

> *For God does not show favoritism. (Romans 2:11)*

Judgment will be dealt out strictly and exactly, justly and fairly by God.

6. God will judge men according to the "light" that He made available to them.

> *All who sin apart from the law will also perish apart from the law, and all who sin under the law will be judged by the law. (Romans 2:12)*

This "light" includes both general moral understanding of right and wrong as well as the specific revelation of the Gospel. The greater the "light" one rejected, the greater his judgment. This principle is stated in Luke 12:

> *That servant who knows his master's will and does not get ready or does not do what his master wants will be beaten with many blows. But the one who does not know and does things deserving punishment will be beaten with few blows. From everyone who has been given much, much will be demanded; and from the one who has been entrusted with much, much more will be asked. (Luke 12:47-48)*

Consider also the words of Jesus in Matthew 11:

> *Then Jesus began to denounce the cities in which most of his miracles had been performed, because they did not repent. "Woe to you, Korazin! Woe to you, Bethsaida! If the miracles that were performed in you had been performed in Tyre and Sidon, they would have repented long ago in sackcloth and ashes. But I tell you, it will be more bearable for Tyre and Sidon on the day of judgment than for you. And you, Capernaum, will you be lifted up to the skies? No, you will go down to the depths. If the miracles that were performed in you had been performed in Sodom, it would have remained to this day. But I tell you that it will be more bearable for Sodom on the day of judgment than for you." (Matthew 11:20-24; cf. Luke 11:31-32)*

Jesus said that the wicked ancient cities of Tyre, Sidon and Sodom would receive a less severe judgment in the Last Day than the cities which heard and rejected His own preaching of the Gospel with signs and wonders.

So, we see that a man is not judged only by his works; he is also judged according to the knowledge of God and truth that he rejected. This has great significance when we consider the sin of the apostate who has known the truth of the Gospel and yet willfully turns from it after obeying it for a time. He turns away from God with his eyes wide open. Awful judgment awaits him. Peter says:

> **Life Application Question**
>
> What will the judgment be of the people in a modern country like America, who have rejected a great deal of light?

If they have escaped the corruption of the world by knowing our Lord and Savior Jesus Christ and are again entangled in it and overcome, they are worse off at the end than they were at the beginning. It would have been better for them not to have known the way of righteousness, than to have known it and then to turn their backs on the sacred command that was passed on to them. (2 Peter 2:20-21)

The Six Judgments of God

Historically, there have been many judgments of God, of both nations and individuals. However, our concern here is with "eternal judgment," the final judgment of men's lives that determines their lots for eternity. In this regard, there are six great judgments of God.

> **Life Application Point**
>
> If you receive the benefits of Jesus' death now, you will never have to pay the penalty for your sins!

1. The judgment of sin at the cross.

   > *"Now is the time for judgment on this world; now the prince of this world will be driven out. But I, when I am lifted up from the earth, will draw all men to myself." He said this to show the kind of death he was going to die. (John 12:31-33)*

   At the cross of Jesus Christ, man was judged for his sin. The results of this judgment were that Jesus died and that believers can live.

   "The wages of sin is death" (Romans 6:23). For divine justice to be satisfied, God demanded a death to be "paid." Our sins had to be punished before we could be accepted by God and restored to fellowship with Him. Jesus died in our place. The holiness of God demanded man's death as the just and righteous penalty for his sins, but the love and mercy of God provided a "substitute" to bear that penalty in man's place. Jesus bore the punishment of our sins in our place and thereby set us free from that punishment.

   Our sin was judged for eternity in the death of the body of the Lord Jesus Christ.

   > *...God [sent] his own Son in the likeness of sinful man to be a sin offering. And so he condemned sin in sinful man, (Romans 8:3)*

2. The judgment of believers at the Judgment Seat of Christ.

   > *For we must all appear before the judgment seat of Christ, that each one may receive what is due him for the things done while in the body, whether good or bad. (2 Corinthians 5:10)*

   > *You, then, why do you judge your brother? Or why do you look down on your brother? For we will all stand before God's judgment seat. (Romans 14:10)*

This judgment is for believers only. It is not a judgment to see if we will be saved; that issue was settled at the cross:

> *I tell you the truth, whoever hears my word and believes him who sent me has eternal life and will not be condemned; he has crossed over from death to life. (John 5:24)*

It is a judgment of our works to determine our eternal rewards. This judgment will result either in the gain or the loss of eternal rewards and blessings, based upon our works from the time of our conversion.

The judgment is described in 1 Corinthians 3:

> *For no one can lay any foundation other than the one already laid, which is Jesus Christ. If any man builds on this foundation using gold, silver, costly stones, wood, hay or straw, his work will be shown for what it is, because the Day will bring it to light. It will be revealed with fire, and the fire will test the quality of each man's work. If what he has built survives, he will receive his reward. If it is burned up, he will suffer loss; he himself will be saved, but only as one escaping through the flames. (1 Corinthians 3:11-15)*

It is clear that the judgment is of the believer's works and not of the believer himself. Even if his works are totally burned up, he will still be saved.

Paul speaks of two categories of the believer's works. On the one hand, there are "gold, silver, costly stones." On the other hand, there are "wood, hay, straw." The righteous works will go through the "fire" of judgment unharmed, whereas the worthless works of the believer will be destroyed.

> **Life Application Question**
>
> This coming judgment should be a great motivation in your life to walk with God in reality. Are there things in your life that need to change?

It is obvious from this that quality of works is more important to God than quantity. Gold, silver and precious stones are rare and come in small sizes and quantities; in contrast, wood, hay and straw are easily found and usually in great quantities.

In judging our works, God will examine several things:

> a) What was the nature of our work? Were we truly obeying God or were we just doing what we chose to do?
>
> b) What was our motive in it? Were we doing it for our own ends or truly for God's glory?
>
> c) How did we do the work? Did we do it in our own strength and wisdom or did we rely upon His power and enabling?

3. The judgment of Israel in the time of Jacob's Trouble.

   After He has regathered them from all nations,

   > *I will bring you from the nations and gather you from the countries where you have been scattered – with a mighty hand and an outstretched arm and with outpoured wrath. (Ezekiel 20:34)*

   God will judge His nation Israel:

   > *I will take note of you as you pass under my rod, and I will bring you into the bond of the covenant. I will purge you of those who revolt and rebel against me.... (Ezekiel 20:37-38)*

   Before Israel will be saved, the rebels will be purged from the nation during

Life Application Point

There is a special blessing for those who pray for Israel to be saved (Psalm 122:6-7). You should pray for Israel daily.

the time of the Great Tribulation. This is also called the "Time of Jacob's Trouble":

> *How awful that day will be! None will be like it. It will be a time of trouble for Jacob, but he will be saved out of it. (Jeremiah 30:7)*

After that judgment, Israel will recognize her Messiah. The whole nation will repent.

> *And I will pour out on the house of David and the inhabitants of Jerusalem a spirit of grace and supplication. They will look on me, the one they have pierced, and they will mourn for him as one mourns for an only child, and grieve bitterly for him as one grieves for a firstborn son. (Zechariah 12:10)*

and be saved:

> *And so all Israel will be saved, as it is written: "The deliverer will come from Zion; he will turn godlessness away from Jacob." (Romans 11:26; cf. Isaiah 66:8; Jeremiah 30; 31:1-11)*

4. The judgment of the Gentile nations.

> *When the Son of Man comes in his glory, and all the angels with him, he will sit on his throne in heavenly glory. All the nations will be gathered before him, and he will separate the people one from another as a shepherd separates the sheep from the goats. He will put the sheep on his right and the goats on his left. Then the King will say to those on his right, "Come, you who are blessed by my Father; take your inheritance, the kingdom prepared for you since the creation of the world."…Then he will say to those on his left, "Depart from me, you who are cursed, into the eternal fire prepared for the devil and his angels."…Then they will go away to eternal punishment, but the righteous to eternal life. (Matthew 25:31-46)*

At the close of the Great Tribulation, when Jesus returns in glory, those on the earth who survive the judgments of Revelation 6-19 will be brought before Him and separated as the sheep and the goats. Only the righteous (the "sheep") who were saved during the time of Tribulation, and whose salvation was expressed by their good works, will be allowed to enter into His kingdom. The "goats" who were not saved will be sentenced to eternal punishment.

5. The Great White Throne judgment of the lost.

> *Then I saw a great white throne and him who was seated on it. Earth and sky fled from his presence, and there was no place for them. And I saw the dead, great and small, standing before the throne, and books were opened. Another book was opened, which is the book of life. The dead were judged according to what they had done as recorded in the books. The sea gave up the dead that were in it, and death and Hades gave up the dead that were in them, and each person was judged according to what he had done. Then death and Hades were thrown into the lake of fire. The lake of fire is the second death. If anyone's name was not found written in the book of life, he was thrown into the lake of fire. (Revelation 20:11-15)*

> **Life Application Question**
>
> If Jesus returns in our lifetime, then you know some people who will stand in this judgment. Are you reaching out to them now that they be saved?

This is the final and ultimate punishment of those who died without Christ. This will take place after the 1000 year period of the Millennium.

The Scripture says that "books" will be opened, and then, "the book of life" will be opened. All who are not found in the book of life will be cast into the lake of fire. All the lost will also be judged according to their works as revealed in the "books," which are presumably the records of their deeds. This indicates that there will be degrees of punishment for the lost.

While all the lost will suffer infinitely – in the sense of eternally – in hell, there are still differing degrees of suffering among them.

Ezekiel 32:17-32 teaches that the wicked are not all treated alike, but rather, there are degrees of punishment for the lost. Many other Scriptures speak of degrees of eternal punishment for the lost:

> *Jesus answered, "You would have no power over me if it were not given to you from above. Therefore the one who handed me over to you is guilty of a greater sin." (John 19:11)*

> *Woe unto you, scribes and Pharisees, hypocrites! for ye devour widows' houses, and for a pretence make long prayer: therefore ye shall receive the greater damnation. (Matthew 23:14, KJV; Cf. 10:14-15; 11:20-24; 23:15; Luke 20:47)*

We shall consider the nature of the eternal punishment of the lost shortly.

6. The judgment of the fallen angels.

   This judgment is prophesied in the Old Testament:

   > *In that day the Lord will punish the powers in the heavens above… (Isaiah 24:21; cf. 27:1)*

   Satan himself will be judged:

   > *And the devil, who deceived them, was thrown into the lake of burning sulfur…They will be tormented day and night for ever and ever. (Revelation 20:10)*

All the angels who took part in the original rebellion against God with Satan will be judged.

> *And the angels who did not keep their positions of authority but abandoned their own home – these he has kept in darkness, bound with everlasting chains for judgment on the great Day. (Jude 6)*

> *For if God did not spare angels when they sinned, but sent them to hell, putting them into gloomy dungeons to be held for judgment; (2 Peter 2:4)*

These angels will be judged by Jesus along with His saints. At one time, when the demons recognized Jesus as the Son of God they cried out, "What do you want with us, Son of God?... Have you come here to torture us before the appointed time?" (Matthew 8:29). "The appointed time" spoken of here is the time of their coming judgment by God when they will be tormented.

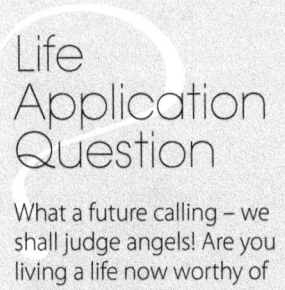

Life Application Question

What a future calling – we shall judge angels! Are you living a life now worthy of such a calling?

That the saints of God will play a part in this judgment is revealed in 1 Corinthians 6:

> *Do you not know that we will judge angels? How much more the things of this life! (1 Corinthians 6:3)*

The Nature of the Eternal Punishment of the Lost

The eternal sufferings of the lost consist in:

1. Exclusion from the presence, favor and fellowship of God.

   > *These will receive the punishment of eternal destruction as exiles from the presence of the Lord…(2 Thessalonians 1:9, Williams New Testament)*

   God is infinite Spirit and is everywhere all at once. Therefore, "exclusion from the presence of God" does not mean there could ever exist a place where God is not (Jeremiah 23:24; Psalm 139:7-8). Nevertheless, it will be Jesus who says to the lost, "Depart from **me**" (Matthew 7:23, KJV; cf. Psalm 5:4-6; Matthew 25:41; Luke 13:27; John 8:21; Revelation 21:27; 22:15), and so this signifies eternal alienation from God and total separation from His manifest presence and blessing.

   This is the essence of the Fall, and it is the worst punishment that could ever come to man – the eternal and irrevocable loss of fellowship with his God. Man was made for God – for fellowship with Him. There will be no greater pain or anguish that comes to ruined mankind than that which results from this loss.

2. The loss of all earthly good, enjoyment and pleasure.

   > *…the mirth of the wicked is brief, the joy of the godless lasts but a moment. (Job 20:5; cf. Job 20:18; 27:8; Psalm 39:6; 49:10, 16-17; Ecclesiastes 2:18; 5:15; Luke 12:20; 16:25; Jeremiah 17:11)*

   While upon the earth, sinful man enjoys much that is good, but it is all only for a moment, a very brief space of time. An instant after death, all the good things he enjoyed in this life, all the social prestige and position he obtained, and all the material wealth he heaped to himself will be gone forever. In eternity, he will discover that the only abiding "wealth" he ever possessed and the only lasting "treasure" he ever laid hold of is the eternal wrath of God (Romans 2:5).

   Another aspect of eternal suffering will be the inward despair and agony of those who are **lost, forever, without hope.** The despair and pain of being utterly and eternally without hope and fully knowing it is unimaginable. Arthur Pink wrote, "unrelieved will be their fearful sufferings; interminable their torments. No means of escape. No possibility of a reprieve. No hope of deliverance...'There is **no peace,** saith my God, to the wicked.' There will be no resting-place in hell; no secret corner where they can find a little respite; no cooling fountain at which they may refresh themselves. There will be no change or variation of their lot. Day and night, forever and ever, shall they be punished. With no prospect of any improvement they will sink down into blank despair."

3. The fire.

> *They will throw them into the fiery furnace, where there will be weeping and gnashing of teeth. (Matthew 13:42; cf. Matthew 5:22; 13:47-50; 18:8-9; 25:41; Luke 3:17)*

The fire is obviously not a physical fire because Satan and his angels, who will suffer there as well, are spirit beings. It is, however, an actual fire except it is a spiritual one; it is a fire of spiritual substance. This spiritual fire will be far worse in its ability to inflict pain and suffering than a natural physical fire. It will be an eternal, undying fire.

> *he too (i.e., everyone who worships the beast, and receives his mark) will drink of the wine of God's fury, which has been poured full strength into the cup of his wrath. He will be tormented with burning sulfur in the presence of the holy angels and of the Lamb. And the smoke of their torment rises for ever and ever. There is no rest day or night for those who worship the beast and his image, or for anyone who receives the mark of his name. (Revelation 14:10-11; cf. Mark 9:43; Jude 7; Revelation 20:10; 21:8)*

> *...be thrown into hell, where their worm does not die, and the fire is not quenched." Everyone will be salted with fire. (Mark 9:47-49)*

In Mark 9:49, the phrase "everyone will be salted with fire" probably means that the unquenchable fire of the second death, instead of destroying as fire usually does, will act like salt and **preserve** in a state of torment and agony. Exodus 3:2 and Deuteronomy 5:23 give examples of how God can make a fire that will burn something and yet not destroy it, but preserve it in a state of burning.

The abode of the lost at present, which is in one region of hades, is a place of torment by fire as well (Luke 16:22-28). The testimonies of a number of people who have had supernatural visions and experiences of both hades and the eternal lake of fire confirm all the above.

4. The lake of fire is a place of extreme anguish and torment.

> *But for those who are self-seeking and who reject the truth and follow evil, there will be wrath and anger. There will be trouble and distress for every human being who does evil...*
> *(Romans 2:8-9)*

Paul says the eternal state of the lost will consist in "trouble" and "distress." The Greek words translated "trouble" and "distress" respectively refer to **outward** affliction and **inner** torment. The suffering will be entire: spiritually, mentally, emotionally and bodily – every faculty of man will experience the severest, acutest agony possible to his heightened senses.

The lake of fire will be a place of the most awful suffering. Jesus referred to the "weeping and gnashing of teeth" of the lost no less than seven times in the Gospels (Matthew 8:12; 13:41-42, 49-50; 22:13; 24:51; 25:30;

> ## Life Application Point
>
> Until you have a correct understanding of the true nature of eternal punishment, the awfulness and the immediacy of the plight of the lost will not grip you as they should; consequently, you will not have a true burden for the lost. Let this truth affect you. This is not theory. This is reality. This is the eternal state of those you work with, of your lost relatives, of your neighbors, of the people you walk past in the marketplace. **Let this affect you!** Let it move you to pray, and to reach out to them.

Luke 13:28). Weeping and gnashing of teeth are extreme expressions of sorrow and anguish.

Those in the lake of fire will be "**tormented**...for ever and ever" (Revelation 14:10-11). The Greek word translated "tormented" in Revelation 14:10 means to "torture" or "torment"; it occurs for the first time in the New Testament in Matthew 8:6: "my servant lies at home paralyzed and **in terrible suffering**." The same word occurs again in Revelation 9:5 where it is said that during the Tribulation, the demonic "locusts" will be given the power to torment with "the **sting** of a scorpion when it strikes a man." This will cause a suffering so intense that men will "seek death, but will not find it; they will long to die, but death will elude them." (Revelation 9:6).

The pains and torments of hell will be far beyond the most excruciating pain that one is now capable of conceiving.

5. The companions.

> ...Depart from me, you who are cursed, into the eternal fire prepared for the devil and his angels. (Matthew 25:41)

All the lost will be there, although not to enjoy the pleasures of sin with one another as many would like to believe. Rather, they will suffer in the presence of one another's agonies and torments. All the lost will be there including the most evil, disgusting and vile people who have ever lived. Satan and his angels and demons will also be suffering in torments there.

6. It is eternal.

> Then they will go away to eternal punishment... (Matthew 25:46)

Those who teach that the lost are either annihilated or ultimately reconciled to God after a time of reformatory suffering are in gross error. (For more information concerning the errors of "Annihilation" and "Ultimate Reconciliation," see Appendix 1 in *The Blood of God* by Malcolm Webber.) This fact is seen in those many passages which teach the **everlasting** nature of the **conscious punishment** of the lost.

> *...others to shame and everlasting contempt. (Daniel 12:2)*

> *...thrown into eternal fire. (Matthew 18:8)*

> *They will be punished with everlasting destruction... (2 Thessalonians 1:9)*

> *...They will be tormented day and night for ever and ever. (Revelation 20:10; cf. 2 Peter 2:17; Jude 7, 13; Revelation 14:11)*

This then, was the place of eternal torment for all men but for the grace of God. The eternal rewards and blessings of the redeemed are inconceivable and inexpressible (Isaiah 64:4), and the eternal punishments of the lost are too!

The Nature of the Eternal Reward of the Righteous

Just as God originally created the heavens and the earth, so He will create new heavens and a new earth, untainted by sin or its effects:

> *Behold, I will create new heavens and a new earth. The former things will not be remembered, nor will they come to mind. (Isaiah 65:17)*

> *But in keeping with his promise we are looking forward to a new heaven and a new earth, the home of righteousness. (2 Peter 3:13)*

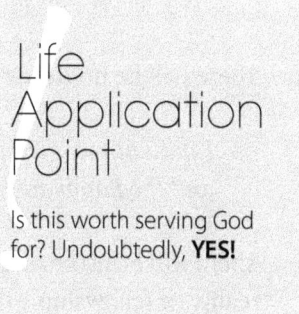

Life Application Point

Is this worth serving God for? Undoubtedly, **YES!**

> *Then I saw a new heaven and a new earth, for the first heaven and the first earth had passed away... (Revelation 21:1)*

God will also create a "New Jerusalem" where He will reign forever:

> *I saw the Holy City, the new Jerusalem, coming down out of heaven from God, prepared as a bride beautifully dressed for her husband. (Revelation 21:2)*

The following are some of the characteristics of the life of the redeemed in this eternal state:

1. We will have unrestricted, personal fellowship with Jesus Christ.

    > *And if I go and prepare a place for you, I will come back and take you to be with me that you also may be where I am. (John 14:3)*

    This will be the greatest thing we will experience for eternity. Gates of pearl, streets of gold and walls of jasper are all wonderful, but they will pale in comparison to the beauty of His face.

    > *And I heard a loud voice from the throne saying, "Now the dwelling of God is with men, and he will live with them. They will be his people, and God himself will be with them and be their God." (Revelation 21:3)*

    > *They will see his face... (Revelation 22:4)*

2. There will be no dead religion there.

    > *I did not see a temple in the city, because the Lord God Almighty and the Lamb are its temple. (Revelation 21:22)*

    There will be no boring ceremonies or rituals – just the joyful, eternal reality of fellowship with God!

3. Those who overcome will reign with Jesus for eternity.

   > ...And they will reign for ever and ever. (Revelation 22:5)

   > if we endure, we will also reign with him.... (2 Timothy 2:12)

   > To him who overcomes, I will give the right to sit with me on my throne, just as I overcame and sat down with my Father on his throne. (Revelation 3:21)

> **Life Application Question**
>
> Why waste your time storing up treasure on this earth, when your eternal inheritance is "all things" with God?

4. We will inherit all things.

   > He who overcomes will inherit all this, and I will be his God and he will be my son. (Revelation 21:7)

5. Everything will be new. The old sin-tainted world will be gone forever.

   > He who was seated on the throne said, "I am making everything new!"... (Revelation 21:5)

6. There will be no more sea.

   > Then I saw a new heaven and a new earth, for the first heaven and the first earth had passed away, and there was no longer any sea. (Revelation 21:1)

   In this life, the seas set the boundaries of the nations, but in the eternal state, there will be no more division or separation between people.

7. There will be no more death, sorrow, crying or pain.

   > He will wipe every tear from their eyes. There will be no more death or mourning or crying or pain, for the old order of things has

> *passed away. (Revelation 21:4)*

Death and suffering are the wages of sin. At the cross, sin was judged eternally, and there will be no more sin or its effects for eternity for the redeemed. For ever and ever there will be no suffering or pain whatsoever!

> *No longer will there be any curse. The throne of God and of the Lamb will be in the city, and his servants will serve him. (Revelation 22:3)*

The final removal of the curse of sin is spoken of by the prophet Isaiah:

> *On this mountain he will destroy the shroud that enfolds all peoples, the sheet that covers all nations; he will swallow up death forever. The Sovereign Lord will wipe away the tears from all faces; he will remove the disgrace of his people from all the earth. The Lord has spoken. (Isaiah 25:7-8)*

The curse of sin, in all its forms, will be gone forever!

8. There will be no darkness.

   > *On no day will its gates ever be shut, for there will be no night there. (Revelation 21:25)*

   > *There will be no more night. They will not need the light of a lamp or the light of the sun, for the Lord God will give them light.... (Revelation 22:5)*

   > *The city does not need the sun or the moon to shine on it, for the glory of God gives it light, and the Lamb is its lamp. (Revelation 21:23)*

   God, Himself, will be the Light of the righteous for eternity.

9. There will be no sin or temptation.

   > *Nothing impure will ever enter it, nor will anyone who does what is shameful or deceitful, but only those whose names are written in the Lamb's book of life. (Revelation 21:27)*

   Only those with righteous natures will be there. There will be no devil or demons there. Eternity will be without sin or temptation of any kind.

   > *But in keeping with his promise we are looking forward to a new heaven and a new earth, the home of righteousness. (2 Peter 3:13)*

10. In the New Testament, a number of "crowns" are described as being part of the believer's reward:

    a) The Crown of Life (James 1:12; Revelation 2:10; 3:11).
    b) The Crown of Glory (1 Peter 5:4).
    c) The Crown of Rejoicing (Philippians 4:1; 1 Thessalonians 2:19).
    d) The Crown of Righteousness (2 Timothy 4:8).
    e) The Incorruptible Crown (1 Corinthians 9:25).

11. We will experience full knowledge.

    > *Now we see but a poor reflection as in a mirror; then we shall see face to face. Now I know in part; then I shall know fully, even as I am fully known. (1 Corinthians 13:12)*

    This does not mean we will know everything. Only God is omniscient, and we shall learn from Him forever. However, there is much that is a mystery to us now that we shall understand clearly then.

12. We will enjoy His glory.

    Father, I want those you have given me to be with me where I am, and to see my glory, the glory you have given me because you loved me before the creation of the world. (John 17:24)

While all believers will be saved, just as there are degrees of suffering among the lost, there will be degrees of glory among the righteous. In 1 Corinthians 15, Paul says that there will be a difference between the glorified bodies of the redeemed. They will all be the same kind of glorified body, but there will be different orders of glory among them.

    The sun has one kind of splendor, the moon another and the stars another; and star differs from star in splendor. So will it be with the resurrection of the dead…. (1 Corinthians 15:41-42)

13. We will serve the Lord forever.

    No longer will there be any curse. The throne of God and of the Lamb will be in the city, and his servants will serve him. (Revelation 22:3)

What a privilege it will be to serve God unhindered with a full revelation of His will, growing in the knowledge of Him forever!

14. We will experience perfect rest.

    Then I heard a voice from heaven say, "Write: Blessed are the dead who die in the Lord from now on." "Yes," says the Spirit, "they will rest from their labor, for their deeds will follow them." (Revelation 14:13; cf. Isaiah 11:10; Ezekiel 34:14-15; Hebrews 4:1)

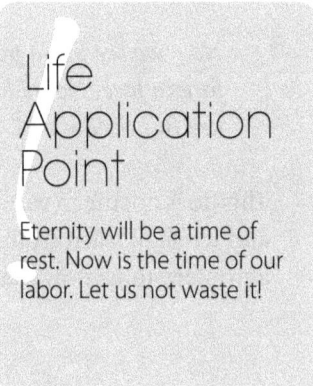

Life Application Point

Eternity will be a time of rest. Now is the time of our labor. Let us not waste it!

This does not mean we will be inactive in heaven because we have seen that eternity will be filled with joyful, fulfilling service to the Lord. However, we will have rest from all the trials, labors and strivings of this life.

15. We will experience total satisfaction.

   Every care will be forgotten, and every need will be supplied. Perfect bliss forever! Jesus truly will be "all we need."

   Some have questioned how we could possibly enjoy total satisfaction in the eternal state when there will be different rewards for the righteous. Will we be tempted to be jealous of someone who receives a greater eternal reward than us? The answer is certainly, "No." For one thing, there will be neither sin nor temptation to sin in eternity. Furthermore, each of us will be entirely satisfied with the reward and degree of glory that we possess. Imagine two glasses of water. Each is a different size but both are full. One glass has more water than the other, but both are as full as they can be. That is what it will be like in eternity. There will be different degrees of reward and glory between the righteous, but each one of us will be "full" and entirely, eternally satisfied.

16. We will experience unspeakable joy.

   > *His master replied, "Well done, good and faithful servant! You have been faithful with a few things; I will put you in charge of many things. Come and share your master's happiness!"* (Matthew 25:21)

   > *The ransomed of the Lord will return. They will enter Zion with singing; everlasting joy will crown*

Life Application Point

In view of this, our response should be:
1. To say with John, "Amen. Come, Lord Jesus."
2. To be faithful to God now.
3. To share the Gospel with others, so they can exchange hell for heaven.

their heads. Gladness and joy will overtake them, and sorrow and sighing will flee away. (Isaiah 51:11)

The greatest joy and enjoyment possible to us in this life is but a shadow of the pure, undefiled, exultant joy we will have for eternity in the presence of God.

Summary

1. All men, saved and lost, will be resurrected, and after their resurrection, they will face judgment.

2. Sin can be against other men, and sin can be against yourself. However, all sin is ultimately against God. God is the One who will judge man for his sin.

3. God is the moral Judge of the universe. He is a righteous Judge, and He will give to everyone his due with unvarying impartiality.

4. The principles of divine judgment are:
    a) God will judge all men.
    b) God's judgment is according to truth.
    c) God will judge every man's deeds.
    d) God will judge the hidden motives of the heart.
    e) God will judge without partiality.
    f) God will judge men according to the "light" that He made available to them.

5. There are six great "eternal" judgments of God:
    a) The judgment of sin at the cross.
    b) The judgment of believers at the Judgment Seat of Christ.
    c) The judgment of Israel in the time of Jacob's Trouble.
    d) The judgment of the Gentile nations.
    e) The Great White Throne judgment of the lost.

f) The judgment of the fallen angels.

6. The eternal sufferings of the lost consist in:
   a) Exclusion from the presence, favor and fellowship of God.
   b) The loss of all earthly good, enjoyment and pleasure.
   c) Inward despair and agony.
   d) The fire.
   e) Extreme anguish and torment.
   f) The companions.
   g) It is eternal.

7. God will create new heavens and a new earth, untainted by sin or its effects.

8. Some of the characteristics of the life of the redeemed in the eternal state are:
   a) Unrestricted, personal fellowship with Jesus Christ.
   b) No boring religion.
   c) Those who overcome will reign with Jesus for eternity.
   d) We will inherit all things.
   e) Everything will be new.
   f) No more sea.
   g) No more death, sorrow, crying or pain.
   h) No darkness.
   i) No sin or temptation.
   j) Believers will receive a variety of "crowns."
   k) We will experience full knowledge.
   l) We will enjoy His glory.
   m) We will serve the Lord forever.
   n) Perfect rest.
   o) Total satisfaction.
   p) Unspeakable joy.

The grace of our Lord Jesus Christ [be] with you all. Amen. (Revelation 22:21)

Review 14

1. What are the two things that no one will ever escape?

   A. _____

   B. _____

2. Complete this verse:

   For we must _____ appear before the _____ seat of _____, that _____ one may receive what is _____ him for the things _____ while in the body, whether _____ or _____. (2 Corinthians 5:10)

3. Please write "true" or "false" beside each of these statements:

   _____ All sin is ultimately against God.

   _____ Sin is just a weakness in man, and God does not mind it.

   _____ God does not punish all sins – just the "really bad" ones.

   _____ God will judge everyone one day.

   _____ God enjoys punishing people for their sins.

   _____ God will only judge us for our outward actions and not for our inward motives.

   _____ God will judge men according to the "light" that He made available to them.

4. Please name the six judgments of God:

    A. _____

    B. _____

    C. _____

    D. _____

    E. _____

    F. _____

5. The eternal sufferings of the lost consist in:

    ☐ Exclusion from the presence, favor and fellowship of God.
    ☐ The loss of all earthly good, enjoyment and pleasure.
    ☐ The inward despair and agony of being lost, forever, without hope.
    ☐ The fire.
    ☐ Extreme anguish and torment.
    ☐ Vile co-inhabitants.
    ☐ It is endless.
    ☐ All of the above.

6. Some of the characteristics of the life of the redeemed in the eternal state are:

    ☐ Unrestricted, personal fellowship with Jesus Christ.
    ☐ No boring religion.
    ☐ Those who overcome will reign with Jesus for eternity.
    ☐ We will inherit all things.
    ☐ Everything will be new.
    ☐ No more sea.
    ☐ No more death, sorrow, crying or pain.

- ☐ No darkness.
- ☐ No sin or temptation.
- ☐ Believers will receive a variety of "crowns."
- ☐ We will experience full knowledge.
- ☐ We will enjoy His glory.
- ☐ We will serve the Lord forever.
- ☐ Perfect rest.
- ☐ Total satisfaction.
- ☐ Unspeakable joy.
- ☐ All of the above. **Hallelujah!**

Answers to Reviews

REVIEW 1
1. The foundation.
2. They did not have the proper foundation in their lives: a personal relationship with Jesus.
3. Jesus. 1 Cor. 3:11.
4. Knowing Jesus personally.
5. Now this is eternal life: that they may know you, the only true God, and Jesus Christ, whom you have sent.
6. All of the above.
7. All of the above.
8. end; means; personal experience.
9. Him revealing Himself to us.
10. wrote; inside; teach.
11. False.
    True.
12. Do not merely listen to the word, and so deceive yourselves. Do what it says.

REVIEW 2
1. hearing; obeying; words.
2. Knowing and obeying the word of God.
3. In the beginning was the Word, and the Word was with God, and the Word was God.
4. Jesus and His Word always agree.
5. True; 1 Tim. 4:16; 1 John 2:24-25; 2 John 9.
   True; 1 Cor. 15:1-2; 2 Tim. 2:16-18; 2 Pet. 3:15-17; 2 John 9.
   True; 1 Tim. 3:15.
   True; Phil. 1:27; 2 Tim. 2:15.
   True; Rom. 16:17;1 Tim. 1:3-4; Tit. 1:9-11; Jude 3.
   False; Phil. 1:9-11; Col. 1:9-10.
   True; 1 John 2:4-5.
   False; John 14:21-23.
6. abiding; continuous; manifest; experienced.

REVIEW 3
1. The Word of God.
2. Ps. 119:89, 160; 12:6; Ezra 1:1; Josh. 22:9.
3. All of the above.
4. True.
5. The Old Testament is the Word of God.
6. Any of the ones cited on pp. 27-28.
7. The Word of God.
8. True.
9. All Scripture is God-breathed and is useful for teaching, rebuking, correcting and training in righteousness.
10. True.
11. contain; is.
12. True.
    True.
    True.
    False. The Word of God is always right.
13. expired.
14. The Holy Spirit.
15. True.
    True.
    False.
    False.
    False.
    True.

REVIEW 4
1. 39; 27; 66.
2. Ezra.
3. A translation of the Old Testament Scriptures into Greek.
4. All of the above.
5. The Old Testament.
6. I tell you the truth, until heaven and earth disappear, not the smallest letter, not the least stroke of a pen, will by any means disappear from the Law until everything is accomplished.
7. True.
   False.
   True.
   True.
   False.
   True.
   False.
   False.
8. this word; light.
   angel; heaven; eternally condemned.
9. The written Word.

REVIEW 5
1. All of the above.
2. It is only the Word of God that produces faith.
   For faith to grow in your heart, you must listen to the Word of God with a heart that is willing to receive and obey. When the Word is "heard" from an attentive and sincere heart, faith will come.
3. True; Jam. 1:18; 1 Pet. 1:23.
   True; John 6:63; Matt. 4:4; Heb. 5:12.
   True; 1 Pet. 2:2; Heb. 5:12-14.
   True; Ps. 107:20; Prov. 4:20-22.
   True; Matt. 8:16.
   True; Ps. 119:130; 2 Tim. 3:16-17.
   False; 1 Cor. 3:19.
   True; 1 Cor. 10:31; Col. 3:17.
   True; Ps. 119:11; 17:4.
   True; Luke 4:8; 1 John 2:14; Rev. 12:11.
   True; John 15:3; Eph. 5:25-27.
   True; 2 Cor. 3:18.
   True; 1 Cor. 2:14.
   True; Acts 1:8; 1 Cor. 2:13.

REVIEW 6
1. Repentance from dead works.
   Faith in God.
   Instruction about baptisms.
   Laying on of hands.
   Resurrection of the dead.
   Eternal judgment.

REVIEW 7
1. Either.
2. To change one's mind.
3. regret; life; change; mind; turn; God.
4. Always.
5. All of the above.
6. more; decision; change; actions.
7. Always.
8. True; Lam. 5:21; Acts 5:31; 11:18; 2 Tim. 2:24-25.
   False; Acts 17:30.

REVIEW 8
1. And without faith it is impossible to please God, because anyone who comes to him must believe that he exists and that he rewards those who earnestly seek him.
2. Faith is the substance of things hoped for.
3. True.
   True.
   True.
   False.
   True.
4. Rom. 4:17-21.
   Luke 1:34-38, 45.
   Luke 5:4-6.
5. difference; word of God; relationship.
6. Rom. 10:10; Matt. 12:34; 2 Cor. 4:13.
7. received; believed.
8. By faith alone.
9. A gift from God.
10. Mark 1:14-15; Acts 20:21.
11. A dead faith.
12. The demons.
13. All of the above.
14. Hear and receive the Word of God.

REVIEW 9
1. The baptism of John.
   Christian water baptism.
   The baptism of suffering.
   The baptism in the Holy Spirit.
2. To immerse.
3. Repentance.
4. repent; example.
5. Suffer for our faith.

REVIEW 10
1. suggestion; commandment; Matt. 28:19; Mark 16:16; Acts 10:48.
2. Repentance.
   Faith.
3. Without delay.
4. True.
   False.
   False.
   True.
   False.
   True.
   False.
5. All of the above.
6. No.
7. Any believer.

REVIEW 11
1. A personality.
2. God.
3. True; Acts 5:3-4; 1 Cor. 3:16; 2 Cor. 3:17.
   True; Ps. 139:7-10; 1 Cor. 2:10-11; Gen. 1:2.

True; Acts 1:8; 1 Cor. 2:4-5; Rom. 15:19.
True; 1 Cor. 1:7.
False; Acts 2:39.
False; Acts 8:5-13; 9:3-6; 19:1-6; Heb. 6:4; etc.
True; Joel 2:28-29; Is. 44:3.
True; Luke 24:49; John 7:39.
4. Acts 8:5-13; 9:3-6; 19:1-6; Heb. 6:4; Eph. 1:13; Gal. 4:6; Luke 11:11-13; etc.
5. All of the above.
6. Speaking in a new language.
7. You can right now.
8. If you then, though you are evil, know how to give good gifts to your children, how much more will your Father in heaven give the Holy Spirit to those who ask him!

REVIEW 12
1. A living, meaningful, effective, Biblical practice.
2. All of the above.
3. To impart a blessing.
   The ministry of healing.
   To receive the baptism in the Holy Spirit.
   To impart spiritual gifts.
   To commission ministries.
   To appoint elders.
   To appoint men for specific acts of service.
4. Mere ritual.
   Extremes.
5. True.
   True.

REVIEW 13
1. Ps. 16:8-11.
2. Job 19:25-27; Is. 26:19; Dan. 12:1-2; Hos. 6:1-3.
3. True.
4. John 5:28-29; 1 Cor. 15:21-23; Rev. 20:5.
5. True.
   True.
   False.
   True.
6. Because He was sinless.
7. True.
   True.
   True.

True.
8. The experience of the guards at the tomb.
   The undisturbed grace clothing.
   The numerous appearances of Jesus after His resurrection.
   The zeal of His disciples.
   The change of the day of rest from the Sabbath (Saturday) to the "Lord's Day" (Sunday).
   The Christian's own personal experience of faith.
9. Dan. 12:2; John 5:28-29; Acts 24:15; Rev. 20:5-6.
10. Old.
    New.
    Old.
    Old.
    New.
    Old.
    New.
    Old.
    New.

REVIEW 14
1. Death.
   Judgment.
2. all; judgment; Christ; each; due; done; good; bad.
3. True.
   False.
   False.
   True.
   False.
   False.
   True.
4. The judgment of sin at the cross.
   The judgment of believers at the Judgment Seat of Christ.
   The judgment of Israel in the time of Jacob's Trouble.
   The judgment of the Gentile nations.
   The Great White Throne judgment of the lost.
   The judgment of the fallen angels.
5. All of the above.
6. All of the above. **Hallelujah!**

Strategic Press
www.StrategicPress.org

Strategic Press is a division of Strategic Global Assistance, Inc.
www.sgai.org

513 S. Main St. Suite 2
Elkhart, IN 46516
U.S.A

+1-844-532-3371 (LEADER-1)

www.ingramcontent.com/pod-product-compliance
Lightning Source LLC
Chambersburg PA
CBHW071152160426
43196CB00011B/2059